LOCATION

R charities

AUTHOR

HATCH

DATE of CATALOGUING

-7 JUN 82

HOUSE OF COMMONS LIBRARY

TO BE
DISPOSED
BY
AUTHORITY

D1582299

# OUTSIDE THE STATE

# Outside the State

Voluntary Organisations in Three English Towns

Stephen Hatch

CROOM HELM LONDON

© 1980 Stephen Hatch
Croom Helm Ltd, 2-10 St John's Road, London SW11

British Library Cataloguing in Publication Data

Hatch, Stephen
    Outside the State.
    1. Volunteer workers in social service -
    Great Britain - Case studies
    I. Title
    361.7'07'22        HV245

ISBN 0-7099-0234-4

Reproduced from copy supplied
printed and bound in Great Britain
by Billing and Sons Limited
Guildford, London, Oxford, Worcester

# CONTENTS

# TABLES AND FIGURES

# ACKNOWLEDGEMENTS

This book is the product of an initiative by the Joseph Rowntree Memorial Trust which first brought into existence the Wolfenden Committee on Voluntary Organisations and then, when the Committee had produced its report, provided the resources for the completion of the research reported here and the establishment of the Voluntary Organisations Research Unit. My thanks are due in particular to Lewis Waddilove in his roles as Director of the Trust, Vice-Chairman of the Wolfenden Committee and Chairman of the Unit's Steering Committee. Roger Hadley has also been involved in the research from the beginning and was directly responsible for the first part of it. In all sorts of ways he has been of inestimable help. I am indebted too to my present colleagues Tilda Goldberg, Ian Mocroft and Ann Richardson; without their advice the work would have had even more imperfections.

Various people provided invaluable assistance in the execution of the research — Brenda Abercrombie, Janet Bell, Alison Chippindale, Jill Cohen, Meg Edmunds, Hilary Latham, Celia Potter, Leslie Turner and particularly Rosalind Howell, who carried out much of the field-work for the Wolfenden Committee. Ruby Bendall patiently turned successive drafts into a final manuscript of the highest typographic quality.

Finally, more than any others I have to thank the many people of the three towns who gave time to describe their work and discuss the role of the voluntary organisations. The book is not intended as a panegyric of voluntary action, but it will be failing its subject-matter if it does not convey how much of it deserves respect and admiration.

Stephen Hatch
Voluntary Organisations Research Unit
Policy Studies Institute

# GLOSSARY

| | |
|---|---|
| ASBAH | Association for Spina Bifida and Hydrocephalus |
| BLESMA | British Limbless Ex-Servicemen's Association |
| CAB | Citizens' Advice Bureau |
| CPAG | Child Poverty Action Group |
| CVS | Council of Voluntary Service |
| DAG | Disabled Action Group |
| DES | Department of Education and Science |
| JCP | Job Creation Programme |
| LEA | Local education authority |
| MGC | Marriage Guidance Council |
| MSC | Manpower Services Commission |
| NOP | National Opinion Poll |
| NSPCC | National Society for Prevention of Cruelty to Children |
| OAP | Old age pensioner |
| PHAB | Physically handicapped and able-bodied |
| PTA | Parent-teacher association |
| RSPB | Royal Society for the Protection of Birds |
| SSD | Social Services Department |
| WEA | Workers' Educational Association |
| WRVS | Women's Royal Voluntary Service |
| YOP | Youth Opportunities Programme |
| YVFF | Young Volunteer Force Foundation |

# 1 AIMS AND METHODS

This book reports on a study of voluntary organisations in three English towns. The study was started for the Wolfenden Committee on Voluntary Organisations. In order to supplement the extensive evidence it received from national voluntary organisations, the Committee needed information about the character of the voluntary sector at the local level. A few of the findings were presented in the Committee's report. [1] After the completion of the report, the research staff of the Committee became the Voluntary Organisations Research Unit, which received financial support from the Joseph Rowntree Memorial Trust in order to extend and complete these locality studies.

Current interest in the voluntary sector reflects a questioning of some of the assumptions that lay behind the rapid expansion of statutory services during the 1960s and early 1970s. Since the oil crisis it has not been possible to assume that the resources devoted to statutory services could any longer be quickly and steadily increased. Even if a moderate increase can be achieved there will continue to be a large gap between needs and demands on the one hand and resources on the other. Hence for any given level of statutory expenditure there is an important question as to how far provision can be extended by voluntary activity.

But it is not just a matter of quantity. Statutory services necessarily have a bureaucratic character, which has been intensified by the recent reorganisations of health, personal social services and local government and the consequential increase in scale of operations. Services of this sort have a number of limitations, as well as certain advantages. These limitations are commonly identified as inflexibility and lack of responsiveness, as tendencies to alienate rather than integrate those they are intended to serve, and to create dependency rather than reinforce natural and informal caring arrangements. Such limitations can in turn be attributed, not only to the inherently rule-bound and departmentalised character of bureaucratic organisations, but also the dominance of the administrators and professionals who staff them, to the lack of community involvement in the services, and so on. Yet progress in the social services is still very widely equated with extensions of statutory services. The caring and support given by families and neighbours and the activities of individuals working voluntarily for organisations nowhere finds a place in the official statistics or in indicators of social welfare. Nor is there an adequate understanding of the effect of the state on these informal or alternative sources of social welfare.

It does not require a radical critique of the role of the state to suggest that alternative patterns for the development of the social services deserve discussion. The subject of the research reported here is the voluntary sector. It and the statutory sector represent two out of altogether four sources of social and environmental care, the other two being the commercial and the informal. The commercial sector consists of the services that are bought by individuals. Its relationship to the statutory sector has been the subject of sustained debate. In contrast, the informal sector has been relatively neglected. Since it will be referred to at various places in this report, a little more needs to be said about it at this stage. It consists of all the services or care that is not provided on a formally organised basis, notably by relatives, friends and neighbours. Despite the growth of statutory services the informal sector remains the main source of care for children and the elderly; while a substantial though unquantified proportion of health care is also carried out informally. No discussion of alternative patterns of development can ignore this very large volume of activity. Moreover, there are trends in other fields which suggest the emergence of a self-service economy. [2] Although not exactly analogous to those operating in the social services, they are indicative of a broader context in which arguments about the role of the state in social welfare can be placed.

This book is about only a part of all the extra-statutory activity. Its aim is not the ambitious one of putting forward a programme for the development of the voluntary sector, or more largely for the social services in general. Rather it seeks simply to describe and appraise what the voluntary sector now is and does. Since the 1940s there has been a dearth of research on voluntary organisations. Hence the foundations are lacking for a forward-looking review that might test existing assumptions and point towards new patterns of development. It is this lack that the book hopes to remedy.

## Preliminary Definitions

The organisations to be studied were defined along two dimensions, following the interests of the Wolfenden Committee. First, it was necessary to say what constituted a voluntary organisation. This is far from straightforward and is discussed more fully in Chapter 2. In brief, voluntary organisations defy definition in terms of essential characteristics. Instead it is necessary to define them as (i) being organisations, not simply informal groups; (ii) not established by statute or under statutory authority and not directly controlled by a statutory authority; and (iii) not commercial in the sense of being profit-making or (like much of the private sector in health and education) being mainly dependent for their resources on fees and charges paid by private individuals.

Second, a limit had to be placed on the fields of activity or need areas to be considered. There are a great many religious and recreational organisations, ones concerned with the visual and the performing arts, occupational interests and the armed services, social clubs, political parties and so on. These meet the definition of voluntary organisations but were not included in the survey, which concentrated on organisations whose activities were related to the social and environmental services. There are five main social services – health, education, social security, personal social services and housing; and the environment comprises both the natural (e.g. wild life conservation) and the built (civic amenities). Also included were organisations concerned with safety and life-saving as well as health (e.g. the Royal National Life-Boat Institution) and with offenders, and generalist organisations like community associations and Rotary clubs with a significant though not exclusive interest in social welfare. The primary interest of some organisations such as churches lies outside these fields, but they may carry on significant secondary activities within them. Where these constituted separately organised entities, like church-run clubs for young people and pensioners, they were included.

## The Three Towns

The surveys reported here seek to present a picture of the voluntary sector as a whole, encompassing all the many organisations in the fields covered. The three towns are described under the pseudonyms of Anglebridge, Forgeham and Kirkforth. Although in some discussions assurances were given that the identity of individuals would be protected, the pseudonyms were not adopted because a lot of highly confidential information will be deployed; rather, by avoiding what could be taken as public judgements on the towns and their inhabitants, voluntary organisations can be discussed more freely and directly, and with less fear of causing offence and raising extrinsic issues.

Two of the towns, *Kirkforth* and *Anglebridge*, were chosen as a pair. Similar in population size and in being the centres of larger non-metropolitan districts, they provided a contrast in terms of recent population growth, economic prosperity and patterns of employment. Kirkforth is in the north-west. With a large proportion of unskilled, low-paid jobs and a low level of car ownership, it lacks the prosperity of Anglebridge without being conspicuously depressed or deprived. The character of the place has some of the dourness of the local stone, open and wind-swept instead of constricted in a narrow valley like many of the northern towns. Its population has been growing only slowly, and there is no lack of a local identity. In contrast, the population of Anglebridge and its surrounding villages has increased by two-thirds in the past two decades, some of it attracted by opportunities for commuting to London. But the growth, the mobility of the population and the location of the town somewhat in the shadow of London have negative effects, to which one of the people we interviewed gave expression:

It's the influx of very young people buying their own homes. It's this peculiar mixture of society . . . . This great influx from London. . .it's changed so much just in the nine years I've lived here. When I first came I knew

everybody in the shops and they knew you, but now it's
just like a London suburb. People keep themselves to
themselves; they don't want to get involved. To me, living
here, it seems like a satellite of something bigger . . .it
doesn't have a core or a belonging.

No doubt many of the residents enjoying a comfortable
suburban existence have little reason to see the town in this
light, and certainly the wealth of voluntary activity does not
corroborate the absence of identity; but the comment conveys
some of the dislocating effects of growth and change that
seemed to be absent in Kirkforth.
  Anglebridge's main local industrial employers are in the
engineering and electrical fields, while in recent years there
has been a growth of office employment, some of it
attributable to the county council which has its headquarters
in the town and some to the movement of offices from
London. In terms of its socio-economic profile the town is
heavily weighted towards white-collar occupations. The
population as a whole is a prosperous one, as evidenced by a
high level of car ownership, if hardly rich. It is also mobile,
but this is not the mobility of rootless single people, or of
immigrants from poorer countries; rather it is middle-class
families moving ahead. This general picture is not one
suggestive of high levels of social need. Numbers of infirm
elderly, of handicapped, of unemployed and of the low-paid
are lower than in the other two towns. Nor was there
evidence of a large-scale housing problem. The more
characteristic difficulty is that of the young wife isolated at
home.
  *Forgeham* constitutes a Midlands metropolitan district. It
has a much larger population that the other two towns, with
more heavy industry and worse housing. A high proportion
are employed in skilled manual jobs, and there is a substantial
ethnic minority population. Like Anglebridge, Forgeham has a
redeveloped and thriving town centre. The spread of pleasant
suburbs on one side of the town contrasts with an extensive,
unprepossessing jumble of heavy industry, council estates,
canals, waste land and elderly Victorian terraces on the other.
And like Kirkforth rather than Anglebridge, it has no lack of
civic pride and identity. Since local government reorganisation
political control of Forgeham has been in the hands of the

Labour Party, but its position is by no means unassailable. The district councils for Anglebridge and Kirkforth, on the other hand, have been safely Conservative, like their county councils.

Table 1.1 presents a brief statistical profile of the towns drawn from the 1971 census. The relationship between the towns and the areas surveyed is discussed more fully in Chapter 3. Here it is important to note that in the case of Anglebridge and Kirkforth the areas studied extended beyond the boundaries of the town as they existed in 1971 to include a substantial rural or semi-rural and middle-class population.

**Table 1.1 : 1971 Census Data from the Three Towns**

|  | Anglebridge | Forgeham | Kirkforth |
|---|---|---|---|
| Total population (thousands) | 58 | 266 | 50 |
| Percentage population aged 0-14 | 25 | 25 | 24 |
| Percentage population of pensionable age | 13 | 18 | 14 |
| Percentage increase in population 1951-71 | 67 | 9 | 9 |
| Percentage households owner-occupiers | 57 | 42 | 59 |
| Percentage households council tenants | 28 | 45 | 25 |
| Percentage households lacking exclusive use of all amenities | 12 | 19 | 15 |
| Percentage present residents with both parents born in the New Commonwealth | 1 | 11 | 1 |
| Percentage households headed by migrant within past 5 years into area | 26 | 7 | 12 |
| Percentage households without a car | 39 | 52 | 58 |
| Percentage females aged over 15 economically active | 46 | 45 | 41 |
| Percentage economically active males in: | | | |
| supervisory and skilled manual jobs | 27 | 43 | 34 |
| semi-skilled and unskilled jobs | 17 | 23 | 30 |

No three towns can adequately encompass or exemplify the full extent and diversity of the towns of this country or for that matter of the voluntary organisation activity in them. A town larger than Forgeham would have been beyond our resources, and within that constraint the aim was to obtain a good geographical spread and a variety of social and economic conditions. It is necessary to ask, but difficult to answer, how far a different choice of towns would have produced an essentially different picture of the voluntary sector. Subsequent research [3] suggests that, like other similar towns, both Kirkforth and Anglebridge have a relatively large number of branches of national voluntary organisations, while Forgeham is the kind of town with relatively few. However, as indicated in Chapter 3, Forgeham seems to have a considerable number of local neighbourhood organisations which were not covered in the research on the branches of national organisations.

One factor which might have influenced the extent of voluntary activity is a history of deliberate efforts, emanating either from an organisation like a council of voluntary service or the local authority, to develop and strengthen the voluntary sector. But none of the towns had a strong CVS, nor are any of the relevant local authorities conspicuous in their efforts to develop the voluntary sector. Another general factor is the level of statutory provision on personal social services. This can be conveyed by the expenditure per thousand population of the three authorities concerned. [4] None of them was an extremely high or an extremely low spender. In terms of the national average, which is strongly weighted upwards by the London boroughs, all are below average. But more specific comparisons are perhaps fairer. In terms of the 47 English and Welsh counties, the authority covering Kirkforth came just within the top ten, while that covering Anglebridge came just within the bottom ten. Forgeham, in relation to the other 35 metropolitan districts, also came just within the bottom ten. The implications of the level of statutory expenditure are unclear, however, since higher expenditure might in some ways stimulate voluntary activity and in other ways discourage it. Thus impressionistic evidence should also be taken into account. A comparison of the three towns with impressions of other places would suggest that each town and its voluntary organisations is of course unique, but not peculiar. There is variation between the towns in their voluntary organisations, some of it interesting and significant, but broadly speaking, in exploring the voluntary sector in each place, we seem to have been digging into a common stratum of structures, understandings and assumptions. This stratum or culture, we would suggest, underlies the whole of the country.

## The Course of the Research

In each town the survey work had two stages. First, while the Wolfenden Committee was sitting, a list of voluntary organisations was drawn up and a postal questionnaire sent to all the organisations identified. This was supplemented by interviews with representatives of individual organisations and with people like local authority liaison officers whose work made them knowledgeable about the voluntary sector and its relationships with local government. The first stage of the survey was carried out in Kirkforth in the summer of 1975, followed by Anglebridge in the autumn of 1975 and Forgeham in the early part of 1976. Two and half years later, after the Wolfenden Committee had completed its report, came the second stage of the study. It had two purposes: to fill the gaps in the information available, due particularly to non-response at the first stage, and to discover changes caused by the formation of new organisations or the death of existing ones. The first stage of the study in Kirkforth was carried out by Professor Roger Hadley, a member of the Wolfenden Committee, and a locally recruited research assistant. In the other places the first stage was conducted by the research staff of the Committee. The second stage of the inquiry was carried out in each place mainly by two local residents who gathered information by telephone, supplemented by letters or visits for people not on the phone.

The thoroughness of the data is greatest in Kirkforth, followed by Anglebridge and then by Forgeham, where because of the size of the place and limits of time and money the more numerous categories of organisations were not all individually surveyed, and the response rate to the questionnaire was low anyway. The implications are explained where relevant in the text.

The reader will naturally want to know whether, within the boundaries chosen for the study, a complete coverage was achieved, since the significance of much of the information reported here depends on the completeness of the coverage. Among organisations known to exist, and excluding the large categories not individually surveyed, by the end of the second stage of the survey, there were only some 2 or 3 per cent about which no information at all had been obtained. But what about the organisations never discovered? One can hardly count something one does not know exists! However, the likelihood of undiscovered organisations can be commented on in the light of the steps taken to detect organisations and the incidence of organisations discovered serendipitously. Anglebridge was fortunate in having a directory of organisations annually updated and issued by the local newspaper. This was supplemented by a good list kept by the public library, and lists of organisations compiled by a standing conference of voluntary organisations and by the county community council. As in the other towns, public notice-boards and the local press were monitored and inquiries were made of knowledgeable individuals. Altogether the chances of an organisation escaping our attention in Anglebridge must be accounted poor. In Kirkforth the available lists were of lower quality. But the main point is that the town was small enough for it to be difficult for organisations to escape the attention of the core of people most actively and widely involved in the voluntary sector.

Forgeham presented the most difficulty, partly because of its size, one result of which was the existence of subsidiary centres and foci for social activity. The library and the local authority public relations section jointly produced a directory. But it was not complete, and was supplemented with information gathered from the social services department, the files of the Citizens' Advice Bureau and inquiries of people with knowledge of particular fields. It is possible that local organisations not seeking to make a public impact and not linked with a group of like organisations may have been missed. Likelihood of omission must have been greater among those that were fading out, or were new and not seeking publicity at their formation. However, by the end of the inquiries, which spanned a period of nearly three years, serendipitous discoveries of organisations seem to have dried up. And given that the second stage of the survey was carried out by people familiar with the areas from being resident there for some years, it seems reasonable to claim that very few organisations were missed.

How the research came to be carried out has already been indicated very briefly, but the impression given so far might seem like that not infrequently conveyed by research reports — that the research process had something of the character of a clockwork train that was wound up and then ran its course, meeting perhaps the occasional obstacle but essentially following a predetermined pattern. In real life, research tends to depart from this rational model; often it could more accurately be described as a crab-wise process of discovery. This is not to say that the rational model should not be aimed at. But particularly where it does not correspond to the reality, the reader deserves an account of the course taken by the research if he is to make a fair judgement of its results.

Certainly this research consisted more of piecemeal improvisation than the smooth unfolding of a grand design. To begin with, when the author appeared on the scene as the senior research officer in the summer of 1975, the Wolfenden Committee had already been sitting for more than six months and wanted evidence and briefing on a variety of subjects. However, there was general agreement that the locality studies should have the first priority, and in order to get them under way Roger Hadley set in motion the first of them in the summer vacation of 1975. The aim was to feed information to the Committee as soon as possible, rather than waiting for the implementation of a developed research programme, the results of which could only be presented to the Committee when many of its judgements had already been formed. Beyond this there was no commitment at the beginning of the research to its completion after the Committee disbanded or to separate publication of the results.

The essence of the research approach — comparative community studies — was agreed from the beginning. But at that time our knowledge of the voluntary sector as a whole, if not of particular bits of it, was scanty, and many of the problems of definition and coverage and the specific questions which the research might answer crystallised slowly as the research developed. The longitudinal aspect of the study was only decided on after the Committee had finished its work. An exploratory study, like this one, is bound to evolve with the progress of the research. Nevertheless more thorough data could have been acquired and better use of it could have been made if more planning had been done at the beginning and if the servicing of the Committee had not made competing demands on time.

Despite these limitations what has emerged is a survey that is both comparative and longitudinal. These features give it certain advantages over most community studies, which examine one place at one moment of time. Thus some judgements can be made about what is and what is not unique to one place and about the direction and rate of change. The research also has the strength of a community study in being able to say something about the whole of the field and such interrelationships as exist between its parts. Conversely, there are many questions about the voluntary sector it cannot answer – those concerning, for example, the motivation of volunteers, the dynamics of different kinds of organisation and the present and potential roles of voluntary organisations in particular fields. All the same, the exercise will have served its primary purpose if, in the light of it, future researchers know better where to start than we did in 1975 and if commentators can no longer justify assertions of complete ignorance about the voluntary sector as a collectivity.

## The Plan of the Book

The fact that voluntary organisations are so numerous and varied often presents those who have to relate to them with considerable problems. These are not infrequently voiced by statutory officials, who feel they are dealing with an incoherent entity. An equivalent problem of coherence faces those who seek to analyse and write about voluntary organisations. Hence the book starts off with an attempt at definition and classification, which forms the substance of Chapter 2. There follow two chapters which present the main body of data gathered during the research. The first of these (Chapter 3) concentrates on the existing situation and the second (Chapter 4) includes evidence from earlier studies to indicate the ways in which the voluntary sector is changing.

Any appraisal of what voluntary organisations do now or might do in the future makes little sense unless it is related to the main form of organised provision, which is the state. Chapter 5 therefore reviews earlier theories about the relative roles of the voluntary and statutory sectors before examining the actual contribution made by voluntary organisations in different fields. It concludes by putting forward two models that serve to identify alternative approaches applicable to the present situation. Chapter 6 then examines the interactions between the sectors. Finally, Chapter 7 returns briefly to the broader themes touched on at the beginning of this chapter.

**Notes**

1.   *The Future of Voluntary Organisations* (Croom Helm, 1977).
2.   J. Gershuny, *After Industrial Society: the Emerging Self-service Economy* (Macmillan, 1978).
3.   S. Hatch and I. Mocroft, 'Factors Affecting the Location of Voluntary Organisation Branches', *Policy and Politics*, vol. 6 (1977), pp. 163-72.
4.   The Chartered Institute of Public Finance and Accountancy, *Personal Social Services Statistics*, 1975-6 actuals (published annually).

# 2 WHAT ARE VOLUNTARY ORGANISATIONS?

Voluntary organisations, it was suggested in the previous chapter, do not share an essential characteristic which marks them out from all other kinds of organisation. Nevertheless it is still necessary to say what they are, and for practical purposes they have to be distinguished by a process of exclusion, by drawing boundaries between them and the other kinds of organisation. Such a pragmatic exercise is necessary for delimiting the field of study and actually carrying out a survey. However, it is not altogether satisfactory or satisfying, since what falls within the boundaries may appear no more than a rag-bag. And it is difficult to say much about rag-bags except that they are rag-bags. Hence, whether it is a matter of purely intellectual coherence or one of developing principles to guide action, an analysis is needed which will establish certain central features of the voluntary sector, if not its single essence. In other words, even if the question 'What are voluntary organisations?' has no simple answer, it is necessary to get beyond an exercise in drawing boundaries on the ground.

The attempt to answer this question determines the shape of this chapter. First, possible candidates for the essential character of voluntary organisations are examined and discarded. Second, the distinctions required to circumscribe the voluntary sector are described. Third, several ways of distinguishing between voluntary organisations are reviewed. A simplified classification is then developed which seeks to pick out some essential sources of variation among them.

One way of looking for defining features of voluntary organisations is to examine the basis upon which people participate in them. Thus one may ask whether there is not something distinctive in their 'voluntariness'. Voluntary organisations may be seen as ones which are formed voluntarily; or as organisations in which people participate voluntarily, in the sense of receiving no financial remuneration. Or perhaps they are organisations which share both characteristics. The fact that an organisation is established voluntarily does separate it from all statutory organisations, but not from commercial organisations. Non-payment of participants is a character of many voluntary organisations not shared by commercial organisations, but, there are numbers of important voluntary organisations, the National Trust and Barnados to name only the largest, which depend very heavily on paid staff. Equally, with these examples in mind, it cannot be argued that voluntary organisations are essentially or necessarily smaller, more informal or spontaneous or non-hierarchical. Hence voluntariness on its own cannot be accepted as a diagnostic feature.

Another possible defining feature is the character of the organisation's objectives. Thus it can be argued that voluntary organisations are all to some degree charitable. The Goodman Committee on Charity Law and Voluntary Organisations [1] posed the question:

> How then can we distinguish charitable objects from other objects? Is it possible to frame the definition which will neatly include every object which ought to be regarded as charitable and as neatly exclude everything which ought not to be so regarded, . . .? (para. 26)

After discussing the two main criteria of benefit to the community and altruism, the Committee concluded that 'we do not believe that it is possible to formulate a definition of this sort' (para. 31). The main obstacle to a definition of voluntary organisations in terms of charitable objectives is the existence of numerous mutual aid organisations. These fall within the common-sense meaning of voluntary organisations, but are often based more on self-interest than altruism and sometimes pursue objectives that the rest of the community would not regard as beneficial.

## The Boundaries of the Voluntary Sector

Hence a more pragmatic approach to the search for

definitions is required. First it is necessary to establish the boundary between the voluntary sector and the informal sector. The key factor here is that an organisation is an organisation at all. An informal group does not usually have a name, but having a name is a necessary rather than a sufficient condition for being an organisation; for example, a group assembled for therapeutic purposes by a professional may have a name, but without some distribution of responsibilities among its members, particularly arrangements for looking after its money, it would not constitute an organisation. Thus having a name, objectives and a distribution of responsibilities or roles among its members seem to be the key features here.

Another boundary is that between the voluntary sector and the statutory sector. The essential question is whether the organisation was established by statute or under statutory authority, or whether a majority of its governing body is appointed on statutory authority. The fact that an organisation is mentioned in or derives power from a statute is not a crucial factor. Thus the NSPCC and the National Trust are both unambiguously voluntary organisations, but the power of the NSPCC to bring proceedings before juvenile courts for the protection of children derives from a statutory instrument based on Section One of the Children and Young Person's Act 1969, while the constitution of the National Trust is enshrined in the National Trust Act 1971. Nor does independence from government yield a particularly useful distinction, since a quango like the Personal Social Services Council may well be able to act more independently than a voluntary organisation entirely dependent on a local authority grant.

The third and perhaps most difficult boundary is that between the voluntary and the commercial or private sector. There are two possible indicators here: one is whether the organisation is profit-making and the other is whether the organisation is dependent on private fees. There can be little disagreement that profit-making excludes an organisation from the voluntary sector. Dependence on private fee-paying is a more stringent criterion. There are a number of organisations, particularly ones providing education and health care, which are not profit-making and may even possess charitable status, but which are mainly dependent for their resources on private fees. Access to the services provided by such organisations is dependent upon ability to pay. The view taken here is that this factor does separate them from those which offer services accessible on the basis of need irrespective of ability to pay. There is a spectrum of organisations which obtain varying proportions of their resources from private fee-paying, charges paid by local authorities on behalf of users of the service and donations. A line can be drawn at the point where a majority of the resources used by the organisation in carrying out its work are derived from private fees.

## Sources of Variety

By the devices indicated above the boundaries of the sector can be located. A more demanding task is to make sense of the variety that lies inside them. A large number of distinctions can be made, most of which may be useful for one purpose or another. Thus one obvious, relatively straightforward basis for grouping organisations is according to their field of activity. This is the approach adopted in the next chapter in presenting evidence about the number of organisations. Similarly, organisations can be examined in terms of their size, which is also discussed in the next chapter, or in terms of their age, which is considered in Chapter 4. However, the essential point to discuss is the purpose which any classification scheme will serve. What is being sought here is a means of understanding the behaviour of organisations. Thus a classification scheme will be useful in so far as it helps to explain what makes them tick, and what affects the part they can play in society. The great diversity of voluntary organisations means that such questions cannot usefully be asked of voluntary organisations as a whole. Indeed discussions of voluntary organisations often reach an impasse because the participants find they are talking about different kinds of organisation, and if one looks hard enough it is not difficult to find evidence to illustrate any proposition about the voluntary sector one cares to name. Hence a typology of some sort is needed before much progress can be made in studying voluntary organisations.

There is an extensive literature about voluntary

associations, much of it stemming from a political science perspective and centred on the debate about pluralism and the distribution of power. A useful and fairly recent review of it is provided by Smith and Freedman. [2] Here, however, the perspective is a social policy one, which makes it possible to focus on a narrower range of organisations.

In his post-war report entitled *Voluntary Action,* [3] Lord Beveridge concerned himself with:

> Action inspired by one or other of two main motives — Mutual Aid and Philanthropy. The first motive has its origin in a sense of one's own need for security against misfortune, and realisation that, since one's fellows have the same unique need, by undertaking to help one another all may help themselves. The second motive springs from . . . the feeling which makes men who are materially comfortable, mentally uncomfortable so long as their neighbours are materially uncomfortable: to have social conscience is to be unwilling to make a separate peace with the giant social evils of Want, Disease, Squalor, Ignorance, Idleness, escaping into personal prosperity oneself, while leaving one's fellows in their clutches (pp. 8-9).

Although many new organisations have come into being and the social climate has changed substantially, Beveridge's distinction remains an important and fundamental one. It finds a reflection in a well known classification of organisations advanced by Blau and Scott, [4] based on asking who are the main beneficiaries of the organisation. They identified four types of beneficiary: the shareholders, the clients, the members and the public at large. From these they derived four types of organisation: business organisations, service organisations, mutual benefit associations and commonweal organisations respectively. Voluntary organisations are to be found among each of the last three. A majority count as service organisations; that is to say there is a category of people in direct contact with the organisation who receive services from its workers. Barnardos is one such organisation and an OAP club would also count as a service organisation rather than a mutual benefit association if the 'members' took no part in running it, if the members were in effect clients. A considerable number of voluntary organisations count as mutual benefit associations. The final category, commonweal organisations, is typified for Blau and Scott by prisons and armies; but in fact there are a number of voluntary organisations with a rather different character that come into this category. The main ones are organisations which seek to promote a cause rather than the interests of their members, for example Friends of the Earth and the CPAG. There is another type of organisation which does not fit very readily into the Blau and Scott classification: that is organisations whose main beneficiaries are neither an identifiable category of individual clients nor the public at large, but other organisations. Here one would place organisations like councils of voluntary service, which the Wolfenden Committee described as 'intermediary bodies'. These were discussed by the Committee at some length since it argued that they had an important role in developing and supporting voluntary action. The usefulness of the Blau and Scott classification is that it identifies one category of organisation, business concerns, which includes no voluntary organisations; and another category, mutual benefit associations, nearly all of which are voluntary organisations. Indeed the only mutual benefit associations one might wish to exclude from the category of voluntary organisations are those like professional associations and trade unions, the membership of which is effectively compulsory. However, the other distinctions seem less germane.

Another dimension of no less importance than the nature of an organisation's beneficiaries is the nature of the commitment of those who carry out its work. This theme is central to Etzioni's analysis of organisations. [5]  He examines organisations according to the basis on which they secure compliance from their participants, and among other distinctions makes one between normative organisations, the involvement of whose participants in the organisation is moral, and utilitarian organisations, the involvement of whose participants is calculative. More crudely, some participants take part because they believe in the organisation, others because it serves their interests. Participants in voluntary organisations are always animated by a mixture of motives, but there is in most of them a strong moral element. This is particularly true of organisations which mobilise volunteers to serve others. These are a clear case of Etzioni's normative organisations. Mutual aid organisations, on the other hand, are mixed. One type of involvement in them is purely instrumental — a member participates because the organisation offers material benefits to him. However, there is a strong normative element in most self-help groups, a conjunction of self-interest and moral imperatives that comes across clearly in Robinson's account of Alcoholics Anonymous. [6]

Where paid staff do the work of the organisation there is bound to be a calculative element in the involvement of the staff, in that they are being remunerated for their work. It may be that in some voluntary organisations which depend primarily on paid staff this is the dominant form of involvement, but most voluntary organisations obtain a stronger commitment from their staff than could be achieved simply on a calculative basis. Nevertheless the predominance of paid staff is likely to have a significant effect on involvement, if only in a negative sense, since employment involves a contract which can be terminated.

A third dimension of variation is according to the basis of authority in the organisation. This way of looking at organisations owes most to Max Weber and provides another fourfold distinction. Some organisations operate on a hierarchical or bureaucratic basis; that is, decisions are made at the top and are passed down through a chain of command which leaves relatively little discretion to those who carry out the operational activities of the organisation. Most large statutory and commercial organisations operate on this basis, but some organisations which rest on this model of authority are to be found in the voluntary sector. These are mainly the large uniformed organisations like the WRVS and the Red Cross. It might be argued that this form of authority is incompatible with voluntary effort, but in view of the numbers that work voluntarily for such organisations it can hardly be maintained that this is so; indeed it would appear to have certain advantages for this kind of activity.

A second basis of authority is the professional; that is, decisions are made on the basis of knowledge and skill, usually acquired by education or training, rather than derived from higher authority. Organisations of this kind leave the front-line worker with a high level of autonomy, as is appropriate in organisations whose operational activities consist of the exercise of professional expertise. In the voluntary sector they are to be found among organisations that rely upon volunteers, like the Samaritans, as well as among organisations that rely on paid staff, like the Family Service Units and the child care agencies. Among the latter, however, as in the large statutory and commercial organisations that depend heavily on professionals, there is often a tension between bureaucratic and professional authority.

A third model of authority is the democratic, where decisions are made collectively by the members of the organisation. There is little scope for this kind of organisation outside the voluntary sector. Within it this form of authority seems particularly associated with mutual benefit associations and those that pursue a cause. However, it also occurs in other contexts, such as the community project run by a small group of paid staff with a strongly held ideology and among the many local organisations that are in effect small groups with a shared commitment.

Finally, there is a basis of authority that can best be described as the personal. This fits organisations where authority rests with an individual or a group on account of their special qualities. These qualities may be inspirational — many organisations revolve around a single charismatic leader — or they may inhere in the social status of the leadership.

Another way of looking at organisations is according to the strategies they adopt to pursue their objectives. Such strategies have a close relationship to the role adopted by voluntary organisations in relation to the statutory services. The most obvious distinction is between organisations that provide a service themselves and those that seek to bring about changes in the policy and practices of other organisations. The latter strategy may be pursued in a more or less conflictual manner, ranging from simply communicating needs to public campaigning and direct action. In between service provision and seeking change in other organisations comes the pioneering project which provides a service that the organisation hopes to see adopted by other agencies.

## A Classification Scheme

Besides Beveridge's basic distinction between the motives of
mutual aid and philanthropy, four dimensions of variation
have now been suggested. Particularly in the case of the nature
of participants' involvement and the basis of authority in the
organisation, these represent ideal types rather than
distinctions clearly applicable on the ground. Moreover, if
all these sources of variation are permutated against each
other simultaneously one emerges with a very large number
of individual categories of organisation. In fact the number is
too great to be of practical help in looking at voluntary
organisations. A more parsimonious scheme should therefore
be of value, one which draws what it can from the preceding
theoretical distinctions and links it to common-sense
perceptions of the ordinary observer.

One basis for such a scheme is to think in terms of the
resources used by voluntary organisations in carrying out
their work. Here one begins with a basic distinction between
organisations dependent mainly on voluntary effort and
organisations dependent mainly on paid staff. The former can
be separated according to the nature of their beneficiaries
into those which seek to help others and those which pursue
the interests of their members. The latter can be distinguished
according to the source of their funds, into those which
obtain most of their resources from donations and charges
and those which are funded predominantly by grants. Figure
2.1 presents these distinctions schematically.

**Figure 2.1 : Who Carries Out the Work of the Organisation?**

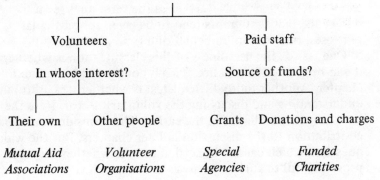

| Volunteers | | Paid staff | |
| --- | --- | --- | --- |
| In whose interest? | | Source of funds? | |
| Their own | Other people | Grants | Donations and charges |
| *Mutual Aid Associations* | *Volunteer Organisations* | *Special Agencies* | *Funded Charities* |

Like all attempts to classify social phenomena, this one does not fit all organisations perfectly and unambiguously. Thus some organisations are hybrids. Some local spastic societies consist mainly of parents of children with cerebral palsy or adults with the condition — these are mutual aid associations. Other branches have a mixture of sufferers and helpers who are not related to them, so that the branch itself is a hybrid. Yet others are unambiguously volunteer organisations, being run by non-spastics for spastics. The national Spastics Society itself operates its services mostly with paid staff and raises its money from private donations and charges for services; thus it is a funded charity. What are being examined in the chapters that follow are the organisational activities taking place in the three towns, so that the classification relates to the local branches or operational units studied, irrespective of whether other parts of the organisation fall into a different category.

Problems also arise with the names chosen for the four categories. The term 'volunteer organisation' does serve to identify the essential character of these organisations, but suffers from being too close to the generic 'voluntary organisation'. 'Mutual aid associations' also depend on volunteers, but the word 'aid' as opposed to 'benefit' does seem to distinguish them from a larger category which includes organisations whose work is done mainly by paid staff. Most voluntary organisations have charitable status; to use the term charities for only a few of them is therefore somewhat invidious, but the term 'funded charities' does seem to convey better than any other the character of this category of organisation. Equivalent objections apply to the term 'special agency'. Nevertheless the term does seem to reflect the fact that grants tend to be given for particular purposes, rather than on behalf of a general cause.

One test of the usefulness of this classification is whether it can be applied in practice. This is considered in the next chapter. Another more difficult test is whether it is useful in understanding and discussing the voluntary sector. Here the proof of the pudding is in the eating. The terms do make some contribution to the discussion in later chapters. But the wider question, which cannot be settled here, is whether they will prove helpful to further analysis and research.

Nevertheless, by way of concluding comments, a few points emerging from the analysis in this chapter deserve to be noted. In terms of the sources of variation noted earlier, mutual aid associations seem to be the most homogeneous category. Thus besides having the members as beneficiaries, they tend to rely upon a mixture of calculative and moral involvement and to depend mainly on democratic supplemented by personal authority. This kind of organisation does not occur in the statutory sector, and there are interesting questions as to how far it can make a distinctive contribution to social welfare.

Volunteer organisations rely essentially on moral involvement, but vary in terms of the character of their beneficiaries and the basis of their authority. In particular there is an interesting contrast between the large hierarchical organisations with a clear national structure and the organisations that are essentially autonomous local groups resting on democratic or personal authority.

Special agencies also show considerable variation in terms of the character of their beneficiaries and the nature of authority within them. Their main feature is that they tend to be particularly beholden to one grant-giving authority. Grants are given in pursuit of the authorities' statutory duties, but usually for activities which the authority does not wish to carry out itself, either because the category of people to be helped is unpopular or because the work to be done requires flexibility and unorthodoxy. But these very features are likely to cause strains between the grant-giver and the special agency.

Funded charities tend to rest on bureaucratic mixed with professional authority. In this they are similar to most statutory social service agencies. The main difference stems from the source of the funds. These are raised from a large number of people, whose decision to give is likely to depend more on the appeal of the cause which the organisation is serving rather than on their knowledge about the effectiveness of the organisation's work. This gives funded charities a large measure of independence, which can be put to good or less good use.

The dominant form of organisation in advanced industrial societies is the large bureaucracy. This is the kind of organisation in which most people earn their living and the instrument for the execution of most public purposes. It depends mainly on the calculative involvement of those who carry out its work and rests on bureaucratic, sometimes diluted by professional, authority. Such organisations have advantages and disadvantages. This is not the place for a lengthy appraisal of bureaucracies, but the contradictions behind many of their disadvantages were analysed by Crozier[7] some time ago. The following quotation summarises a more extended discussion:

> By and large, the common underlying pattern of all the vicious circles that characterize bureaucratic systems is this: the rigidity of task definition, task arrangements, and the human relations network results in a lack of communication with the environment and a lack of communication among the groups. The resulting difficulties, instead of imposing a readjustment of the model, are utilized by individuals and groups for improving their position in the power struggle within the organisation. Thus a new pressure is generated for impersonality and centralization, the only solution to the problem of personal privileges.

Thus, whatever the inescapable need for bureaucracy, it is at best a mixed blessing, not something to be relied upon exclusively. The voluntary sector is not without its bureaucracies, but perhaps the most significant conclusion to emerge from this dicussion is that it encompasses a great variety of organisational types. These are a reservoir of alternative forms for mobiiising and expressing common endeavour.

## Notes

1.  *Charity Law and Voluntary Organisations* (Bedford Square Press, 1976).
2.  C. Smith and A. Freedman, *Voluntary Associations: Perspectives on the Literature* (Harvard University Press, 1972).
3.  Lord Beveridge, *Voluntary Action* (Allen and Unwin, 1948).
4.  P.M. Blau and W.R. Scott, *Formal Organisations: A Comparative Approach* (Routledge and Kegan Paul, 1963).

5.   A. Etzioni, *A Comparative Analysis of Complex Organisations* (The Free Press, 1961).

6.   D. Robinson, *Talking Out of Alcoholism: the Self-help Process of Alcoholics Anonymous* (Croom Helm, 1979).

7.   M. Crozier, *The Bureaucratic Phenomenon* (University of Chicago Press, 1964), p. 196.

# 3  THE NUMBER AND VARIETY OF ORGANISATIONS

Counting is a basic and elementary skill. Hence one might imagine that establishing the number of voluntary organisations in a given area would be a straightforward, if uninteresting, task. Indeed, surveys which seek to do this are not uncommon, yet little cumulative knowledge emerges from them. It is virtually impossible to say whether there are more or fewer organisations in a given geographical area or in a given field of activity, or to point to areas that are well or poorly endowed with voluntary organisations. This is because the accurate counting of voluntary organisations is more difficult and laborious than might be imagined. Not only are some of them elusive to discover or contact; often it is hard to say whether what exists constitutes a separate voluntary organisation. Hence exact definitions have to be arrived at and applied before comparable and cumulative evidence can be established.

There are a lot of other questions that need to be asked about voluntary organisations besides their numbers. Nevertheless an exercise in getting the facts straight is an essential part of the present work. Thus the first part of this chapter is concerned with the number of organisations. The distinctions made in the previous chapter between different types of organisation are then used to indicate how the organisations vary among themselves. This leads on to illustrations of different kinds of organisation, which occupy the last half of the chapter.

Before looking at the figures a definitional point not dealt with in the last chapter needs to be mentioned. At what point does one organisation become separate from another? For the purposes of this study we certainly wanted to count branches or operational units of national organisations as separate entities. However, where a national organisation was represented by a single person, as not infrequently happens with fund-raising agencies, that person was not counted as a separate organisation. It was more difficult to tell at what point two parts of the same organisation became separate. Thus some organisations have separate sections for a younger or older age range, for example Multiple Sclerosis and Crack which is aimed at younger MS sufferers. These we counted as separate where there seemed to be a committee which did not have to have its decisions ratified by another committee, and where it managed its own finances.

The number of organisations is summarised in the table below, which represents the gathering together of the primary material with which this report is concerned.

**Table 3.1 : The Number of Organisations by Field of Activity, 1977/8**

|  | Forgeham | Anglebridge | Kirkforth |
|---|---|---|---|
| Handicapped and Disabled |  |  |  |
| Blind and deaf | 6 | 6 | 6 |
| Other specific | 7 | 10 | 14 |
| General | 17 | 15 | 6 |
|  | 30 | 31 | 26 |
| Mental Health | 5 | 2 | 2 |
| Elderly |  |  |  |
| OAP clubs | 60[a] | 28[b] | 12[a] |
| Others | 5 | 4 | 4 |
|  | 65 | 32 | 16 |
| Families, Children, Play |  |  |  |
| Playgroups and mothers of toddlers | 70 | 25[b] | 9[a] |
| General | 11 | 5 | 14 |
|  | 81 | 30 | 23 |
| Counselling, Rights, Advice | 6 | 7 | 4 |
| Health and Safety | 6 | 8 | 6 |
| Education | 1 | 2 | 2 |
| Housing |  |  |  |
| Tenants' associations | 31[b] | nil | 1 |
| Other, mostly special needs | 9 | 4 | 4 |
|  | 40 | 4 | 5 |
| Environment | 4 | 8 | 6 |
| General Voluntary Effort | 19 | 13 | 8[a] |
| Generalist Neighbourhood Organisations | 21 | 11 | 2[a] |
| Ethnic | 12 | nil | 1 |
| Miscellaneous | 4 | 5 | 5 |
|  | 294 | 153 | 106 |

Notes:  a. Probably an understatement, see below
         b. Probably an overstatement, see below

In describing in more detail the organisations summarised in the table, the reader may gain the impression of a myriad of organisations, endlessly variable from one area to another, adhering to no coherent pattern and expressing an almost infinite range of individual commitments and concerns. This is indeed an aspect of the truth. But the reader might go on to think that very little of general significance could be said about all these organisations, and that certainly they could hardly form part of any coherent or purposive effort to meet needs in a comprehensive way. Later on we shall attempt to say why such propositions are invalid. However, we begin by showing what a lot of loose threads there are.

Organisations for the handicapped and disabled can be divided into three groups. Those for the blind and deaf number the same in each place, and in each place an organisation for the deaf employs at least one specialist social worker, whereas social work for the blind has been assimilated into the social services department (SSD). About half these organisations are basically local social clubs, plus in each town a branch of the Deaf Children's Society, in two of the towns a recently established Talking Newspaper and in Forgeham a blind institute providing housing and workshops as well as varied social activities. The other organisations dealing with specific conditions are distributed between the towns in inverse proportion to the population, with fewest in Forgeham. A few are simply fund-raising organisations. Others are primarily a source of mutual support to sufferers or their parents. Four organisations, Spastics, the Association for Spina Bifida and Hydrocephalus (ASBAH), Multiple Sclerosis and the British Diabetic Association occurred in each town, with the residue of organisations forming a diversity symptomatic of the uneven incidence of voluntary action.

Of the organisations for the disabled generally, half of those in Forgeham are essentially social clubs for elderly people, whereas in Kirkforth there is only one such organisation. The others include two branches of the British Limbless Ex-Servicemen's Association (BLESMA), two Disabled Drivers' Associations, friends of homes and organisations for sport and recreation for the younger disabled, there being as many as six of this sort in Anglebridge. There were only two organisations that could be described unambiguously as pressure groups – a small Disablement Income Group (DIG) committee in Anglebridge and a growing Disablement Action Group in Forgeham. Thus the overall pattern varies considerably, with the emphasis in Forgeham on clubs, in Kirkforth on specialist organisations and in Anglebridge on activities for the younger disabled. Also included in this category are organisations for the mentally handicapped, one of which exists in each town.

Comparatively speaking, organisations dealing with mental health are extremely thin on the ground. Alcoholics Anonymous occurs in each town, but there is only one organisation in Kirkforth directly concerned with mental health generally and no organisation in this category in Anglebridge. Forgeham, however, has a dedicated association which provides hostel accommodation for ex-patients.

The two most numerous types of organisation deal with people at opposite ends of the age range – clubs for old age pensioners and playgroups. Unfortunately for the purposes of exact comparison, as explained below the OAP clubs and playgroups in Kirkforth included only those in the town itself; and we were not able to locate all the OAP clubs in Forgeham. Over forty of these clubs were affiliated to Age Concern and we were told that a good many more were not. Hence the figure in the table is an estimate. In Anglebridge there were two special problems relating to definitions and the coverage of our inquiries. The first concerns 11 groups of wardened flatlets for the elderly, where the wardens had been told to establish social clubs for the residents. Some, but not all, of these were essentially groups run by the warden, which would not count for our purposes as self-standing voluntary organisations. However, we could not readily distinguish these from the more autonomous ones, so the whole of this group has been included. The second problem concerned the playgroups; conveniently these are registered and recorded by SSDs, so that there are good lists available. However in Anglebridge, nearly all the playgroups are not true voluntary organisations since they are run by one person who charges a fee. The charge often does little more than cover costs, but the mothers do not run the group. None of the groups in Kirkforth were of this kind, but we suspect that some of those in Forgeham were. All have been included because of the difficulty of drawing a dividing line, but the unwarranted expansion of the Anglebridge figures should be remembered.

Apart from the OAP clubs, organisations specifically for the elderly were few in number. Each town had its Age Concern, which ran a considerable variety of services. Besides this, many of the activities of the general voluntary help organisations and of the neighbourhood care schemes are in fact directed towards the elderly, but because the elderly are not their exclusive concern they are listed separately.

In contrast with Kirkforth and for no obvious reason, organisations for families, children and play are sparse in Anglebridge. Besides playgroups only two organisations in this category were to be found in each of the three towns — the Pre-school Playgroups Association and the Save the Children Fund, the latter being essentially a fund-raising organisation. The variation between the towns is partly a matter of different levels of voluntary activity in this field, partly of different organisations meeting the same kind of need. Thus branches of Gingerbread existed in Anglebridge and Kirkforth, while in Forgeham there was instead a One Parent Social Club. Organisations for widows were included under this heading; in Kirkforth these were represented by a branch of Cruse that came into existence between our two inquiries, while in Forgeham there is a fast-growing branch of the National Association of Widows. In Anglebridge, on the other hand, no such organisation existed.

Counselling, rights and advice organisations present a more uniform pattern. The Citizens' Advice Bureau (CAB), Marriage Guidance and Samaritans occur in each of the towns. The remaining organisations are accounted for by Friends of the Samaritans and of Marriage Guidance, a women's centre in Kirkforth, a branch of the Child Poverty Action Group (CPAG) and two neighbourhood advice centres in Forgeham.

Voluntary effort in the health field may appear more limited than in fact it is because of the inclusion of specialist organisations in the handicapped and disabled section. What are left are Hospital Friends, St John's Ambulance and the Red Cross, most of which deploy large numbers of volunteers. In addition Anglebridge has a Hospital Radio; and consumer-orientated organisations took the form of a recently formed branch of the National Association for the Welfare of

Children in Hospital (NAWCH) in Kirkforth and a branch of the National Childbirth Trust in Kirkforth and Forgeham. A home safety committee and two fund-raising branches of the Royal National Lifeboat Institution were also placed in the health category, while in Forgeham an organisation had been set up to raise funds for establishing a hospice for which the Area Health Authority could not provide the money.

The number of organisations in the educational field is extraordinarily low. They represent simply branches of the Workers' Educational Association (WEA) in each town, and one (at the first stage of the inquiry two) branches of the Campaign for the Advancement of State Education. In addition in Kirkforth a free school had a fleeting existence between the two phases of our study. However a considerable number of relevant organisations were not placed in this category. First, community associations which in Forgeham receive very active support from the local education authority were placed with other neighbourhood organisations. Second, parent-teacher associations (including 'friends of the school' organisations) and clubs for young people were not thoroughly surveyed in each town. This was because of lack of resources and because the Wolfenden Committee did not actively concern itself with education. However, they were fully studied in Kirkforth, where there proved to be 11 parent-teacher associations (PTAs) in the 22 schools located in the town, and a total of 25 youth organisations. These ranged from numerous small groups related to churches via Scout and Guide troops to a couple of voluntary clubs employing full-time staff. The population of the area served by these organisations was 50,000, which gives some idea of the extra organisations that would have found a way into the study if it had extended fully into the education field in each town.

In numerical terms the tenants' associations in Forgeham dominate the housing field. Though something of a shadow army, this represents a rapid growth in numbers between the two surveys, partly in response to a greater local authority recognition of them. The other housing organisations are all concerned with special needs, and indeed in Forgeham people in these organisations had come together to form an informal pressure group. Each town had a branch of the Abbeyfield

Society, but otherwise it was a matter of different organisations meeting more or less the same range of needs, including those of battered wives, addicts, vagrants and ex-offenders.

The number of organisations concerned with the environment seemed to be in inverse proportion to what the population had to complain about. Thus heavy industry had blighted large parts of Forgeham, but without raising an environmental counter-blast. What each town had was a civic society and a recently formed branch of the Friends of the Earth. These are supplemented in Anglebridge and Kirkforth by action groups with more specific objectives. In relation to the natural as opposed to the built environment, each town had a branch of the Ramblers' Association and Anglebridge and Kirkforth a branch of the local county naturalists trust.

The large ethnic minorities of Forgeham have brought into existence a variety of organisations to meet their own special needs. The organisations counted here are ones primarily concerned with social and material welfare; if the primarily religious organisations had also been included the number would have doubled. The largest organisation is the Council for Community Relations which, not counting Manpower Services Commission (MSC)-funded projects, employs a dozen staff. The others range from a Muslim welfare association to a hostel and advice service for black youths.

The generalist organisations are headed by the Women's Royal Voluntary Service. Certainly this is the largest in terms of the number of people involved in its work. But the great majority of organisations in this category comprise branches of Rotary, Soroptomists, Toc H and Lions, all of which devote a part of their energies to good works, often in support of a local voluntary organisation. In addition, the Salvation Army in Anglebridge makes a major contribution to community service. This category is the one into which councils of voluntary service would be placed. In Kirkforth there was an insecurely funded council but neither of the other two towns had one. In Anglebridge there was a county community council mainly orientated towards the rural areas. Associated with it is a small volunteer bureau which has been included in these figures. Mention should also be made here of a community transport service in Forgeham.

Generalist organisations covering specific neighbourhoods are few in number in Kirkforth, but are represented by a scattering of community and residents' associations in Anglebridge, mostly on the newer estates. Also included in the Anglebridge total are three newly established community care schemes. Community associations form a majority of the generalist neighbourhood organisations in Forgeham and cover perhaps half of the borough. In addition there are half a dozen, mostly recent, neighbourhood care schemes.

## The Ratio of Population to Organisations

The population of Forgeham is more than twice that of the other two towns. Yet Table 3.1 showed that the number of organisations for the disabled was much the same in each place. Judging by the SSD registers, this is not because there are proportionately fewer handicapped persons in Forgeham. In contrast, there are many tenants' associations in Forgeham, while Anglebridge and Kirkforth have only one between them. As shown by the figures in Table 1.1 this is not because the two smaller towns lack council estates. Thus the incidence of voluntary organisations shows wide variations. If these are to be examined systematically, it is necessary to adjust the figures to allow for the differences in population.

When the prevalence of characteristics pertaining to individuals or to the work of statutory agencies is being studied, it is relatively easy to arrive at an appropriate population base. That is more difficult with voluntary organisations. Some do aim at geographical boundaries for their work which follow those of the relevant statutory authority, adopting what is called 'coterminosity'. But some voluntary organisations operate on a neighbourhood basis, in the sense of drawing their participants from a small area, usually within walking distance of their meeting-place, for example, playgroups, tenants' associations and clubs for the young and old; while others may follow local authority boundaries if they constitute a natural catchment area, but will let in people from further away if they want to join. An added complication was brought about by the fact that these studies began shortly after the 1974 local government reorganisation, when some voluntary organisations were still responding to the new situation. It would have been more satisfactory if localities had been chosen for these studies which were exactly coterminous with the boundaries of the new authorities. However, the research began in rather a piecemeal way and in the first place to be studied, Kirkforth, the old boundaries were adopted for the study area. But whatever boundaries had been chosen, the problem of organisations which covered a wider area and of organisations which straddled the boundaries would not have been resolved.

In adopting an actual population base for the making of comparisons Forgeham offers the least problems. The area chosen was that of the metropolitan district with a population of 263,000 in 1977. The study there attempted to include all relevant organisations carrying on activities within the boundaries of the district. In addition, organisations covering an area wider than the district were included if they organised activities in Forgeham for Forgeham people.

In Anglebridge the area studied comprised the town itself and the contiguous urban areas. These contained 95,000 people out of the district's total population of 130,000. The area containing the other 35,000 people is made up of villages, some of them large commuter ones. Some of the Anglebridge organisations recruit a few of their members from these villages, and though county-wide organisations based in Anglebridge were excluded from the survey unless they carried on activities specifically for Anglebridge people, there are some organisations that attracted members living outside the boundaries of the district. As a county town without any larger towns nearer than ten miles, Anglebridge is a favourable location for voluntary organisations. This needs to be remembered in interpreting the figures presented in this chapter. But the local authority boundary does not seem a much better cut-off point than a somewhat larger or smaller area. Hence 95,000 has been chosen as the population base for this area.

In Kirkforth the gap between Kirkforth itself, the area thoroughly surveyed, and the wider area covered by many organisations active in the town is too great for a single population base to be acceptable. Thus the new district contains, as well as Kirkforth itself, a seaside resort with a

population almost as large as Kirkforth, which provided a
separate focus for some voluntary organisations like Rotary
which operated at a level above that of the neighbourhood.
Hence two figures have to be used, one of 50,000 for
organisations serving Kirkforth only and the other of 124,000
for organisations with a wider catchment area.

When differences due to population size have been allowed
for, there remain a variety of specific differences between the
towns which can be seen as the result of unique or chance
factors, and also a more general pattern. The general pattern
emerges when neighbourhood organisations are distinguished
from ones covering the whole of the area. The resulting
figures are shown in Table 3.2.

Table 3.2 : **Organisations in Relation to Population**

|  | Forgeham | Anglebridge | Kirkforth |
|---|---|---|---|
| (a) Neighbourhood Organisations |  |  |  |
| Number | 187 | 64 | 24 |
| Relevant population base (thousands) | 263 | 95 | 50 |
| Organisations per 10,000 | 7 | 7 | 5 |
| (b) Other Organisations |  |  |  |
| Number | 107 | 89 | 82 |
| Relevant population base (thousands) | 263 | 95 | 124 |
| Organisations per 10,000 | 4 | 9 | 7 |

Neighbourhood organisations comprise pensioners' clubs,
playgroups, tenants' associations, community associations and
other bodies with a limited catchment area. The figures show
a fairly even distribution between the towns; but when it is
remembered that the number of pensionsers, clubs and
playgroups in Anglebridge has been inflated by the inclusion
of organisations which on a stricter definition would have
been excluded, it seems that the prevalence of neighbourhood
organisations rises a little with the size of the town. This
makes sense; the smaller the town the less the need for
separate organisations for different parts of it. In addition,
neighbourhood organisations have received more deliberate

encouragement in Forgeham. The staff of the local authority have supported community associations and playgroups there, and have been ready to listen to the tenants' associations. Nevertheless, whatever the part played by deliberate encouragement, it is notable that neighbourhood organisations were relatively more numerous in the most working-class of the towns.

The other, primarily local-authority-wide organisations show a more uneven distribution. In particular there are proportionately fewer in Forgeham. Participation in voluntary organisations tends to decline with social class, and there seems to have been relatively less deliberate encouragement for borough-wide as opposed to neighbourhood voluntary organisations. Also some of the more specialist organisations may operate at a West Midlands rather than a Forgeham level. Looking at it the other way round, in terms of the large number of organisations in Anglebridge, the town is middle-class in character, and, as stated earlier, tends to be the base for organisations serving a larger population than that indicated here. These are some of the underlying factors that seem to be relevant in explaining the differences.

Two other studies serve to set this evidence in a wider context. Newton [1] attempted to count the voluntary organisations in Birmingham and Cousins [2] those in Bromley, Lambeth and Lewisham. The coverage of both studies was considerably wider than this one, but within the fields examined here the number of organisations per 10,000 population seemed to be approximately as follows:

| | |
|---|---|
| Birmingham | 8 |
| Lewisham | 9 |
| Bromley | 9 |
| Lambeth | 5 |

Comparisons are obviously subject to differences in classification and in thoroughness of coverage, the effect of which is likely to be an understatement of the numbers in the Newton and Cousins studies. Nevertheless Lambeth, the most working-class of the places examined, stands out as having few voluntary organisations at the time Cousins collected his data. The other places would not appear to be very different from Forgeham with its 11 organisations per 10,000.

## Level of Participation

Involvement in voluntary organisations and voluntary work takes a variety of forms and, apart from the paid staff, the extent of a person's involvement may vary from what amounts to a heavy part-time job to just helping for an hour or two on the annual flag day. Thus it is very difficult to work out how much voluntary effort is deployed by all the individual organisations. The organisations themselves often do not know exactly how many helpers they have, and few have a good idea of the time each person gives. However, since the level of involvement in voluntary activity is of obvious significance for this report, an attempt was made to find out how many people were actively involved in the work of each organisation, as well as the total membership. In many cases we could equate active participation with committee membership. Sometimes this is because the organisation consists of little else than the committee. In other situations, as with social clubs, the participation of the membership means simply attending meetings or activities. But with the WRVS, for example, a large number of members may be regularly involved in delivering meals on wheels, operating a trolley service and so on, and this we treated as active involvement. Quite apart from difficulties of applying definitions of voluntary involvement across a very varied range of organisations, the information supplied by the organisations is not of uniform reliability. We suspect that organisations are inclined to exaggerate the number of their adherents.

In the light of all these qualifications only a general order of magnitude can be arrived at for the number of active participants. The actual estimates are 4,000 in Forgeham, 2,500 in Anglebridge and 2,000 in Kirkforth. This represents between 2 and 4 per cent of the population aged over 16. The NOP survey carried out for the Wolfenden Committee reported that 8 per cent of the population aged over 16 claimed to have done voluntary work in the preceding week, and 15 per cent in the preceding year. [3] The NOP survey covered voluntary work for statutory organisations, work not under the auspices of any organisation and activity connected with young people and schools. None of these come into the figures for the three towns. Making some allowances for work with young people and schools, it appears that the active participants in voluntary organisations amount to about half the proportion saying to the NOP that they had done voluntary work in the previous week. This seems not unlikely.

While discussing numbers of people, the paid staff of voluntary organisations should not be ignored. The major employers in the voluntary sector are in fact a residential college for the handicapped and a home in Kirkforth and four residential establishments of different kinds in Forgeham. But these establishments serve national or regional needs rather than local ones, and it would not make much difference if they were sited, say, twenty miles away. Hence the following table refers only to the employees of the locally orientated voluntary organisations included in Table 3.1. In addition the part-time employees of playgroups have been omitted, as also staff seconded by the local authority in Forgeham to work with voluntary organisations. In each place full- or part-time staff were employed by the Citizens' Advice Bureau, Age Concern, organisations for the deaf, and organisations catering for special housing needs. In addition the Kirkforth Council of Voluntary Service had taken on six people with funds from the Manpower Services Commission by the time of the second stage of the inquiry; while in Forgeham the Crypt described later in the chapter had 15 people employed on this basis, and the Community Relations Council and associated organisations some 20 full-time staff, some of them also on MSC funding. The overall position was estimated to be as follows:

**Table 3.3 : Numbers of Paid Staff**

|  | Number of Organisations employing at Least One full-time Worker or Equivalent Part-time | Total Full-time Staff | Total Part-time Staff |
|---|---|---|---|
| Forgeham | 16 | 63 | 22 |
| Kirkforth | 8 | 16 | 20 |
| Anglebridge | 8 | 9 | 24 |

**The Variety of Organisations**

Several dimensions of variation were discussed in the last
chapter. In terms of size and structure, from the perspective
of these locality studies voluntary organisations appear
predominantly as small local groups. In very broad terms the
essential elements of the picture are these. Most of the
voluntary organisations covered by the study had a nucleus
of under 20 active participants. Sometimes this nucleus
constituted the whole of the organisation, which at one end
of the spectrum might amount to no more than one
individual with a few adherents. In other cases the nucleus
was associated with a larger number of members who
supported its work without actively participating, received
services from it or attended its functions. Thus the
membership of the larger youth clubs, of a few of the
pensioners' clubs and of several of the hospital friends
exceeded 100. But not all the local organisations were a
nucleus with or without a less active following; a few mobilise
large numbers of volunteers to provide services for others. In
each place the number of WRVS helpers and of Samaritans
exceeded 100, with the WRVS in Anglebridge having as many
as 400 members. The St John's Ambulance and the Red Cross
in two of the towns also had over 100 members. Indeed
St John's in Forgeham reported nearly 500 members. Scouts
and Guides apart, this was the highest figure among the
organisations surveyed. However a considerable proportion of
the members of the Red Cross and St John's are cadets or
others learning first aid, so as far as the role of members is
concerned they come somewhere in between the clubs and
the service-givers. Another measure of size is the number of
paid staff. In these terms the largest voluntary organisations
were the residential homes. Apart from them, Table 3.3 above
shows that only a few organisations employed anybody.

Although the great majority of voluntary organisations at
the local level are largely autonomous groups with very
limited financial resources, most of them are linked with
national associations. Seen from the national level, with all
the local branches subsumed into the single national
organisation, the size of voluntary organisations is less puny.
Whether it makes sense to look at them like this depends in

part on the relationship between the local and the national parts of the structure. In some cases the local branch exists to support the work of the national organisation. This is unambiguously true of organisations that raise money for research, as for cancer, or for providing a service organised on a national basis, as with Guide Dogs for the Blind. In other cases the main purpose of the organisation is pursued through the activities of the local branches, as with Alcoholics Anonymous and most of the mutual aid organisations and such service-giving organisations as Hospital Friends. In these circumstances the national HQ tends to be small and to concentrate on linking and servicing the local groups. A third situation is also common, where the purposes of the organisation are pursued through a combination of national and local activities. Thus most of the work of the Red Cross in this country is carried on through the county branches and local centres, but these make a contribution to the national HQ for its international work. A more even balance exists with many of the organisations concerned with specific handicaps or diseases. Their purposes include both raising money for research and/or specialised national services and also helping the sufferers locally. The question of the right balance between local and national can be a source of tension with such organisations.

The previous chapter advanced a fourfold classification of organisations, and the illustrations that follow will be arranged according to that classification. First, though, the number of organisations in the four categories deserves attention. It is not possible to classify all the organisations accurately. All the same, the orders of magnitude, in relation to the organisations included in Table 3.1, can be suggested. These are better than no attempt at quantification, but should be treated with caution.

In Anglebridge and Kirkforth the proportions were remarkably similar. About half the organisations were volunteer organisations; about a fifth were clearly in the mutual aid category; and a further fifth were either hybrids between mutual aid associations and volunteer organisations or ones where the distinction could not be made on the basis of the information available. The remaining handful of organisations were divided fairly equally between special agencies and funded charities. Forgeham had another pattern. There nearly half the organisations were mutual aid associations; nearly a quarter were volunteer organisations; another quarter were either mutual aid associations or volunteer organisations or hybrids; and among the remainder, which depended mainly on paid staff, special agencies exceeded funded charities. The difference between Forgeham and the other two towns is largely attributable to a factor noticed earlier — Forgeham's large number of neighbourhood organisations, most of which operate on a mutual aid basis.

The pages that follow offer illustrations of the differing organisations that are to be found within the four categories. As well as serving to give some flesh to the so far rather abstract definitions, they should in a more general way convey something of the flavour of the voluntary sector.

## Volunteer Organisations

Volunteer organisations can be subdivided in various ways. Some of them mobilise volunteers for a range of activities that varies according to local circumstances. Well known examples are the WRVS and the Red Cross. They tend to be large, account for a considerable proportion of all voluntary work and have the mobilisation of volunteers as their primary function. With others like Rotary and Soroptomists and church-related organisations, social service is secondary to a primary professional or religious function. In contrast, many volunteer organisations are much more specific. 'Friends' organisations come into existence to support particular statutory or voluntary agencies; while Samaritans, most purely fund-raising organisations and groups providing particular services like clubs for the handicapped are also expressions of commitment to specific causes.

The Salvation Army is an organisation in which social service is a product of a broader religious commitment. In the Salvation Army context the Anglebridge Corps is a strong one and gives a lot of emphasis to community service. The Major and his wife who head the Corps, for all the exiguous level of their remuneration, count as full-time employees. They play a crucial part in the Corps, but apart from them its work is carried out on a voluntary basis.

The Corps has a modern purpose-built centre not far from the town centre, which acts as the base for an extensive range of activities. These include a weekly meeting for the Silver Threads, about 250 pensioners who come for singing and entertainment; a psycho-geriatric club twice a week for whose members meals, handicrafts and transport are provided; a playgroup two afternoons a week; once a week a group for handicapped children; meetings for mothers and toddlers; and with the support of other churches in the town a night shelter. These activities are open to the community at large, but the numerous youth activities are directed more towards those with a commitment to the Army.

The members of the Army in Anglebridge number some 300. All are expected to be active in one way or another, and the Corps is expected to be self-sufficient financially, both as regards the remuneration of its officers and the other activities it undertakes. It does get a little help from the social services department for the expenses of the psycho-geriatric club, and the district council made a contribution to the capital cost of the new centre. Like other volunteer organisations, the Corps has problems with maintaining the reliability of its voluntary efforts and with covering the expenses of its volunteer drivers. Nevertheless the extent of its activities is an impressive expression of voluntary commitment.

Volunteer organisations may not be fragile to the same extent as mutual aid associations, but they do face characteristic problems in maintaining the commitment of their participants. This can take the form of unreliability and simply a falling away of members, or there may be a deflection of goals so that satisfying the needs of the volunteers takes precedence over achieving the objectives of the organisation. The Army deals with this by insisting on a high level of religious commitment translated into a disciplined organisation, given expression in uniform and ranks – a solution perhaps more effective than the secular philanthropy of most voluntary organisations. The Major joins with statutory agencies and other voluntary organisations in identifying social need in the community and working out ways of meeting the needs so identified. The psycho-geriatric club illustrates a recent initiative that followed from this process. Working under this kind of guidance, the risk of volunteers continuing with an activity congenial to them but not of great relevance to the needs of the community seems to be obviated.

The WRVS in Kirkforth is another example of a volunteer organisation mobilising a large number of people and carrying on an extensive range of activities. Founded like other branches of the WRVS in 1938 to mobilise women for the war effort, after the war it had to rethink its role and began to develop services for old people. From this point the services have grown to an extent which can best be conveyed by a list of present activities: three luncheon clubs and one afternoon club for old people, three hospital tea-bars and one for visitors to the prison, ten trolley shops in hospitals and residential establishments, a domiciliary library for the housebound, an 'orthopaedic hostessing service' at the hospital, a clothing and bedding depot for families in need, and a children's holiday scheme. In addition, the WRVS maintains a stand-by role in case of national or local emergencies. Meals on wheels were once undertaken by the Kirkforth WRVS, but are now the responsibility of Age Concern.

The total number of voluntary helpers is well over one hundred. Most of them are middle-aged and above, so the WRVS can be seen as a medium for the active retired helping those who are now less active. But the main problem seems to be finding enough volunteers. More work could be done if there were more helpers, and in particular it is difficult to find younger people who nowadays tend to move on to paid employment. The success of the organisation in Kirkforth owes a great deal to its organiser, who has been involved since its formation and is now in her seventies.

There are trends that seem to be working against the longer-established volunteer organisations. The increasing proportion of married women in paid employment is reducing the pool from which many voluntary workers have traditionally been drawn. At the same time declining religious commitment and the inclination to prefer styles of organised activity less formal than the uniforms and ranks of several of the main volunteer organisations seem to be eroding some of the organisational supports. Thus difficulty in recruiting volunteers was a common refrain in discussions of problems faced by organisations of this kind.

The growth of volunteer bureaux during the past decade and the efforts devoted during the same period to mobilising young volunteers can be seen as attempts to extend the pool from which volunteers are drawn. Emphasising the appeal of particular causes, very evident in the work of the many volunteer organisations that concentrate on fund-raising, represents an alternative way of eliciting voluntary effort; while the current promotion of neighbourhood care is a newer form of drawing on existing specific commitments, in this case to the locality.

## Mutual Aid Associations

Mutual aid associations are represented in our studies by some of the organisations for the disabled and the elderly, by playgroups, by Alcoholics and Gamblers Anonymous, by tenants' and community associations and by some of the environmental and ethnic organisations. The Homebound Disabled Fellowship in Kirkforth is one example. It has a membership of 40 physically handicapped people, plus 20 helper members, nearly all of whom are close kin of one of the handicapped members. Formed in the 1950s, the organisation celebrates its founder with a commemorative plaque. Membership is stable, with death or departure to a home being the main reason for people ceasing to be members. Thus despite the rule that people cannot join once they are past sixty, most of the members are pensioners.

Its main activity is a weekly evening meeting in the county council's smart new day centre. The function of these meetings is social; members with various degrees of mobility and capacity to communicate sit round tables chatting and playing cards or dominoes. Not infrequently additional entertainment is arranged, ranging from bingo or a film show to a performance by a local dramatic society. Most months too there is a coach outing to somewhere like Blackpool or the Lake District, and at Christmas a special party is organised.

Some members take part in the daytime activities of the centre and may participate in other voluntary organisations. But for quite a number the Fellowship is practically their only source of social activity, and one of the few occasions when they get out of the home. Companionship and recreation are thus the main things that the organisation offers its members, things of great value to isolated and sometimes stigmatised people. Beyond this there is an element of psychological support from joining in activities with other disabled people, supplemented by visits, get-well cards and phone contact if a member is too ill to come to meetings.

The Fellowship was founded before the concept of welfare rights became popular, and this is not a topic with which it has concerned itself. However, along with other organisations for the disabled, it does participate in periodic meetings with the divisional SSD, at which topics like the organisation of the meals on wheels service are discussed. These the secretary described as useful.

A major problem faced by the Fellowship, as by other organisations of the disabled, is transport. Some of the members are in wheelchairs and many cannot be brought to meetings by relatives and friends, so special arrangements have to be made. The Fellowship has acquired its own minibus, which is driven by volunteers, and also borrows an ambulance. Although there is a Voluntary Vehicle Service which helps the Fellowship, along with other local voluntary organisations, making sure that all the members can get to the meetings is a constant headache for the secretary. Funding is less difficult. The SSD makes a small grant, and though the membership subscription is a mere 30p per annum, special fund-raising events supported by other organisations in the town bring in additional revenue.

The running of the organisation is the responsibility of a committee of 15, half of them disabled people themselves, with a lot of the work devolved on the secretary. Perhaps the biggest issue facing the organisation is the introduction of new blood — how to find people who will take on responsibilities which the existing officers are finding increasingly heavy.

The pattern of activities adopted by the organisation seems to be successful in meeting some of the needs of elderly handicapped people; but it does not appeal very much to younger people with more ideas and energy who are needed to keep the organisation alive. A lot of hard feelings were caused by the suggestion that another organisation for the disabled ought to be set up. Nor does the Fellowship have a sense of there being a wider set of issues affecting the disabled as a whole, over which it ought to join with other organisations in seeking change.

Another mutual aid association is the Phobic Society, also in Kirkforth. The organisation was brought into existence by a phobic who had her condition largely under control, after reading an article in the *Guardian* about the Phobic Society. This led her to contact a handful of people locally suffering from agoraphobia.

The problem causes sufferers to try to cover up their condition, and this meant that the main problem of the organisation was in making contact with other phobic sufferers in the area. It is an aspect of their difficulties that they are both scared of taking steps towards outside contacts and reluctant to admit their condition. Because of this intermediaries are important. So the founder took leaflets and posters from the national society round to doctors' surgeries, but was never able to get past the receptionist. No referrals came from this source. Only the Samaritans made any referrals.

Meetings of the half-dozen or so members were held in each other's homes about once a fortnight. They were taken up with discussions of difficulties and progress since the last meeting, and accounts of the odd situations members sometimes got themselves into, often ending in a good laugh. Besides which there was simple social chit-chat. This information was gathered in the first phase of the study of Kirkforth. Two and a half years later the organisation could not be traced, and we were told that the founder had moved away from the area.

A third example of a mutual aid association is the Disabled Action Group (DAG) that came into existence in Forgeham between the first and second stages of our inquiry. Most of the other organisations for the disabled in the town are occupied with social activities for the elderly and handicapped, not dissimilar to the Homebound Disabled

Fellowship described above, and have been in existence for some time; indeed the name of one recently defunct organisation — Johnson's Cripple Fellowship — conveys the archaic flavour that persists in some of these organisations. But the DAG has adopted a bolder and broader remit, being concerned with the position of the disabled in society and the provision society makes for them.

The founder and moving spirit of the organisation formerly held a senior post in social services and was confined to a wheelchair as the result of a car accident. Unlike some, he refused to be demoralised by his disability and has devoted himself to campaigning with and for those with less vigour and capability than himself. The group started in a small way following correspondence in the local paper about the government's motability scheme and the trike. Its first major project was a survey of the accessibility of public buildings to disabled people. This involved enlisting the co-operation of children from a number of schools, who in teams of three (two pushing and one sitting in a wheelchair) tested out shops, offices, public toilets, etc. The findings were published with the help of the social services department and gained a Jubilee award which now hangs in the borough's new day centre. This was a breakthrough in terms of public recognition. The founder has been co-opted on to the social services committee and similar surveys are being carried out in neighbouring authorities. But this progress has not been without its difficulties — the Charity Commission at first objected to the inclusion of 'action' in the name of the organisation, and the local Rotary felt it was political. And success has not been achieved without attracting some resentment from other voluntary organisations for the handicapped. It is partly these mutual jealousies and partly the town's endemic parochialism that seem to have prevented the creation of an umbrella organisation for the disabled.

Members of the group now number over one hundred and pay a subscription of 12p a month. They are predominantly middle-aged and have a wide variety of disabilities. Some thirty attend the monthly meetings which are given over to discussion of the business of the organisation. The group has officers but no committee, so any member can join in discussion and decision-making. Only about a dozen take on responsibilities, which now include fund-raising for a trust for young disabled as well as campaigning activities.

Here therefore is an organisation of the disabled for the disabled which in a short space has made a significant impact. The founder has a powerful and challenging rationale for his work. In his view the disabled can be their own worst enemy; re-learning how to live requires very positive attitudes, since professionals sometimes brainwash the disabled into accepting what they think are the norms. It is up to the disabled themselves to reject the inferior status accorded to them by society.

The strengths and problems of mutual aid associations in the social services field are related. On the one hand it is hard to sustain commitment among people whose own personal problems are likely to absorb a lot of their energy, and may limit their capacity for any kind of action. On the other hand, in so far as the sufferer surmounts or learns to cope with his difficulties, the motivation for participation in mutual aid may be reduced. It seems to take an unusual person to translate a preoccupation with his own problems into effective and continuing action on behalf of others in the same situation. These people certainly exist, and they play an important role in all types of voluntary organisation; but as with the Kirkforth Phobic Society, mutual aid associations have particular difficulty in surviving their departure, and as organisations seem to suffer an inherent fragility. The strong commitment to its special ideology and rules demanded by Alcoholics Anonymous, and the procedures used to elicit it, can be seen as a successful attempt to overcome this fragility as well as a way out of alcoholism.

There are mutual aid associations outside the social services field, notably trade unions and professional associations, whose membership constitutes a high proportion of those eligible and which are generally much stronger as organisations, often because membership becomes virtually compulsory. Their characteristic problem is ensuring that the active leadership and paid professionals do serve the interests of and remain accountable to the large passive membership. With the social services organisations apathy is expressed in not even joining; those eligible are often thinly scattered and the proportion who join tends to be low. Their national organisations are not fragile like the local branches, but the link between the national headquarters and the branches is often tenuous –the branches pursue a largely independent existence. Indeed, as with the spastics, in some ways it makes more sense to see them as different kinds of organisations, with the headquarters having more of the character of a funded charity, or possibly in the case of those that receive grants from central government departments of a special agency, servicing a penumbra of local branches.

On the positive side the sharing of problems, evident in the Phobic Society, and the rejection of a stigmatised identity, illustrated in the work of the Disabled Action Group, are things difficult to bring about except on the basis of mutual aid. The Homebound Disabled Fellowship seemed to exhibit less in the way of special mutual aid characteristics, except for the involvement in the organisation of a number of close kin. This might well have been lost if equivalent activities had been arranged by a volunteer organisation or a statutory body. In addition, like other kinds of organisation, mutual aid associations may provide services and campaign for change.

## Special Agencies

These organisations are much less numerous than those in the two preceding categories. They seem to be represented particularly by schemes for caring for the single homeless and by projects with a community orientation, including ones serving young people and/or ethnic groups.

The continuing significance of religious commitment as a source of the impetus behind voluntary organisations is not confined to volunteer organisations like the Salvation Army. The Abbey Trust in Anglebridge is an offshoot of the Anglican diocesan social welfare agency. It runs four hostels — in its terminology houses with guests — and aims 'to provide residential care and rehabilitation' for people who could be described as social rejects — ex-prisoners, addicts, young people rejected from home, unmarried mothers and so on. Though benefiting from a considerable amount of voluntary help, the running of the hostels is carried on by people for whom financial support is obtained from the Home Office, the DHSS and the local SSD. Thus it counts as a specialist agency, although changes in the basis on which it is financed could easily turn it into a funded charity.

The story of the organisation is very much that of one man's powerful Christian commitment to helping the most deprived and outcast, which started off by taking people into his own home. The Trust was formally established in the early 1970s in premises provided by the Church. Thereafter it went through a period of insecurity, with great difficulty in obtaining secure financial support in the absence of recognition from the statutory authorities. But after three years this recognition was achieved and the financial problems have now largely disappeared. It is easy to see how the founder would have appeared unconventional and unprofessional to the staff of statutory organisations, more so even than most voluntary organisations seeking to establish themselves in this field. However the need for the services the Trust provides, the lack of other agencies willing to take on this kind of work and the special quality of what it has to offer have become accepted, aided by the decision to employ a qualified senior social worker to take charge of the running of the hostels.

The Trust aims to provide a Christian family setting. In the words of the founder and chairman:

> the organisations I have been engaged with for many years are made up of one hundred per cent Christian staff and helpers. I would not wish it to have been other than this, and believe that at least for my part, without the knowledge of the love of God and the real working of the Holy Spirit, these schemes would not have functioned. . . It is possible that there are somewhere, non-Christians strong enough and with enough mental equipment to carry out the same work — for our part however, we would not like to take on the task without the certainty that God is with us.

Not only is Christianity important for the commitment of the staff, it also informs the nature of the care that is provided:

> the love that God gives is the love of a soul irrespective of the characteristics of its owner. Such love does not look at

the person in need with the attitude that he or she has got themselves into a mess through their own fault, and thus, should get out of the mess by their own efforts. God's love teaches us that all of us are faulty material.

The uncommitted observer would no doubt react with scepticism to claims of this kind and look for scientific evaluations that would test the Trust's approach. But independent of any Christian commitment or systematic evaluation, it is evident that the hostels do function and do provide for people with severe problems. Moreover the shared commitment is an important part of what makes them function and makes possible a kind of enterprise that would be less easy to mount in the more neutral and bureaucratic setting of a statutory agency.

Special agencies are also prominent among the great variety of statutory and voluntary projects now being directed at the problems of inner-city areas. The Crypt in Forgeham illustrates one such agency. It began in the 1960s when the town's main Methodist church decided to use its basement for a youth club, and before long appointed a full-time youth leader with financial support from the LEA. The church itself is a monumental tribute to the religious commitments of the late Victorian era. It is still well patronised, but the building has become something of a white elephant; crumbling and costly to run, the movement of the residential population away from the town centre has left it without a clear neighbourhood to serve. Instead, with the development of the youth club, it has come to fulfil a widening range of not specifically religious functions for people who come into the town centre.

In addition to young people with some link with the Church, the club attracted a number of others with a diversity of needs and problems, from drugs to homelessness to crime. Responses to these led to a variety of activities based on the Crypt. It continues as a youth club, and has managed to remain a multi-ethnic enterprise, rather than becoming, like so many 'multi-racial' clubs, black-dominated. Associated with it is a PHAB club that meets weekly.

Important among the additional functions taken on by the organisation in recent years is a counselling and advice service. This caters for large numbers of people with an informality that increases the accessibility of the service. In character it seems to be somewhere between a CAB and the Samaritans, with emphasis upon counselling support. One offshoot has been the establishment in two short-life houses of hostels for young people who have become homeless. The most recent major development has been the establishment of a Youth Opportunities Programme Unit. Staffed by three workers, at the time of the second survey it had placed a handful of young people in a variety of social service situations, with the prospect that these numbers would be greatly extended in the near future. There were in addition a number of young people working directly for the Crypt under other forms of Manpower Services Commission (MSC) funding.

The resources to sustain all these activities come from a variety of places and are a tribute to the entrepreneurial skills involved in building up an enterprise of this kind. The church provides the premises; the local education authority funds the two full-time youth and community workers and also pays the part-time youth leaders who work in the evenings; the SSD contributes to the maintenance of the premises and to a fund for helping individuals in need; also through the SSD an Urban Programme grant has been obtained to employ a person to work in the drugs field; the YOP staff are supported by the Manpower Services Commission; and a policeman has recently joined on a one-year secondment aimed at improving understanding between the police force and the ethnic minorities.

The whole project is very much the creation of its director, who has been with it since it was a small youth club. He has found himself close to a growing range of inner-city problems, and has been active in creating greater public awareness of them; identifying ways of alleviating them and seeking out and where necessary campaigning for public funds. Forgeham has a good share of the problems found in ethnically mixed inner-city areas, but has not been so forward as some places in seeking solutions to them. Now there is growing up a critical and articulate voluntary sector that is creating a new dimension to inner-city politics. While careful to avoid close identification with a political party, the leaders of these organisations recognise the need to lobby and campaign for causes that may find little expression through the main political parties. At the same time they are social entrepreneurs running projects which, unconstrained by bureaucracy of their own making, can respond with speed and flexibility to new situations.

The characteristic problems of mutual aid associations and volunteer organisations are to do with recruiting and sustaining the commitment of members. Relationships with statutory services certainly affect their work and are often very significant. But with special agencies these relationships become of central importance, because the salaries of the project staff are dependent on grants. Hence special agencies have always to be persuading either the professionals or the politicians or both that their work deserves support. With the Abbey Trust it was essentially the statutory professionals who had to be convinced, partly because the probation service and social security are not accountable to and thus constrained by local politicians. But with the Crypt, as with most other inner-city enterprises, both politicians and professionals have to be persuaded that the needs the project is concerned with ought to be recognised and that the project is a suitable vehicle for meeting some of them. Thus agencies of this kind are firmly in the political arena; their success is dependent on their skill in mobilising support at the local level. For their part, as they recognise that special agencies can play roles they cannot take on themselves, the statutory authorities become anxious about accountability and knowing how to judge what the agencies are doing.

The prominence of special agencies in providing for the homeless and in the inner cities generally has been noted. Other important examples are intermediary bodies like councils of voluntary service (CVS), advice services and a variety of community projects. The Kirkforth CVS provides an illustration of the difficulties such agencies can face. It was formed in the early 1970s, and shortly before the first Kirkforth survey had scraped together enough money, mainly by way of small local authority grants, to employ a part-time secretary in the person of a retired administrator. But he quite quickly resigned. After an interregnum, and with the help of the county community council, resources were obtained from the Manpower Services Commission to employ six young people. But the MSC's Job Creation Programme did not allow individuals to be employed for more than twelve months, and at the time of the second survey another group of young people was about to be taken on, also with funds from the MSC. As well as administering the CVS, they were running a volunteer bureau, producing a newsletter, supporting a community project and exploring a variety of potential initiatives. But they lacked the experience and understanding to convince the local authorities, who were the only possible source of longer-term funding for full-time staff, that a CVS was really needed. Hence further funds were not obtained, and by the time of writing the organisation had ceased to function.

Some special agencies are a channel for commitment likely to be frustrated in a more neutral, bureaucratic setting; others cater for people or provide kinds of treatment too unpopular to be welcome as a direct statutory responsibility; others have the advantage of speed, flexibility and smallness of scale; yet others can be run in a manner more acceptable and accessible to people who may not trust statutory authorities; and some possess all of these characteristics. But organisations which possess these kinds of advantages are often unstable. Whether because of the intractable problems they deal with, or because of the insecurity of their basic position, they run a risk either of collapsing or of following a familiar path towards greater bureaucratisation. And as they become more bureaucratic they are likely to gain in reliability, but also to lose some of the advantages attributable to smallness of scale and staff commitment.

**Funded Charities**

The local branches of national charities which concentrate on raising funds for the charity have been treated as separate entities and thus rank as volunteer organisations. Otherwise the funded charities were represented in our three towns by six residential establishments, which for the most part were meeting regional or national rather than local needs, and thus had little connection with local social services. In addition there was a blind institute in Forgeham. The NSPCC was also active in each area, but mainly in the form of an officer who covered an area wider than any of the three towns.

Of these establishments the one in Kirkforth run by the Spastics Society underwent an interesting transformation between the two surveys. Initially a training centre for imparting vocational skills to young people with cerebral palsy, by the time of the second survey it had become a college providing one- and two-year courses for some sixty young people drawn from the lower ranges of ability and with varying degrees of physical handicap, from the chair-bound to the fully mobile. Very few of them are ever likely to hold normal jobs; and instead of the vocational training in specific skills that has traditionally been the staple diet of further education for the handicapped, the emphasis in the college course is on personal and social development, on reducing the constraints of the handicap and on learning to live as full a life as possible. In this respect the college represents a new departure in further education, embodying basic re-thinking about the curriculum, and has recruited a group of professionals committed to this goal.

The college is attractively situated in modern buildings on the edge of the town. The students are drawn from all over the country and the running costs are covered by fees paid on their behalf by local authorities. The capital costs were met by the Spastics Society, and the college principal is accountable to the directors of the Society. He has a large measure of autonomy, the only controls on him being essentially budgetary ones; though in addition the college has to satisfy the DES inspectorate. However, should the college not succeed, it could expect to follow the same path as its predecessor the training centre, to be closed with a despatch unlikely to be found in the statutory sector. There is no local management or advisory committee and the college's connections with the local community are not strong; a group of volunteers help with the educational activities, students from the local university come on placements and a Friends organisation exists.

Essentially the role of the college is national, not local. Whatever benefit it may bring to the relatively small numbers for whom it can provide places, it will have to be judged also for its contribution to the development of further education for the handicapped. In this context it represented a professionally run, pioneering enterprise that was the product of thinking about a special problem at a national level, the initiative of a dynamic charity that was happy to allow plenty of scope for innovation.

## Some Conclusions

The information presented in this chapter confirms the point that there are few, if any, essential characteristics shared by all voluntary organisations. One significant consequence is that there are not a great many statements that can be made about the sector as a whole. The different elements of it have to be examined and understood separately.

The test of the classification put forward in this chapter is how far it facilitates this task. In the first place, it is likely to be helpful only if organisations can be allocated to one category or another without too much difficulty. In practice most of the local organisations could be so placed. The largest problem lay between volunteer organisation and mutual aid associations. It arose partly from the paucity of the data. But even with much fuller information there would still have remained a number of hybrid organisations, though few in proportion to those which were unambiguously in one category or the other. Nevertheless it must be admitted that there is something of a continuum, rather than a clean dividing line, over which the extent to which the beneficiaries were involved in running the organisation did not necessarily seem to make a great deal of difference. The same situation seems to apply in varying degrees to the other boundaries between categories. For example, the three Citizens' Advice Bureaux included in the study all had at least one paid organiser, but depended mainly on volunteers. In other places, though, the CAB has become dependent mainly on paid staff and thus a special agency. The interesting question, which this study cannot answer, is how this transition from one category to another affects the work of the organisation, for example its independence from the local authority. The relatively small number of organisations covered by our study that could be described as special agencies or funded charities makes it difficult to generalise about the boundaries between them and other categories. However, again the area of ambiguity does not seem large in relation to the whole.

The second and more substantial test of the classification scheme is whether it enhances understanding of the voluntary sector. More precisely, to what extent can statements be made about the individual categories that cannot be made about voluntary organisations generally? This study was not designed as an analysis of particular categories of organisation, so that the question cannot be answered definitively here. However, it is possible to suggest insights and hypotheses arising from the classification that deserve further examination, and issues that can be clarified with the aid of it. The following discussion is intended to be illustrative, not exhaustive.

Volunteer organisations and mutual aid associations both depend on mobilising individuals to participate in their work, and major organisational issues relate to this. In the last few years growing attention has been directed to volunteering. Although the members of mutual aid associations are also engaged in voluntary activity, the word volunteering tends to be used in practice to mean helping others, and usually implies a formally organised context as distinct from informal caring. Writing about volunteers has tended to be directed at their deployment — how they are recruited, what they can do, their relationship to professionals and so on — and tends to view the phenomenon as primarily a matter of individual behaviour. This is not invalid, but it ignores what can be a significant component in the situation — the organisational context. The Salvation Army is a case in point; the primary commitment of its members is to the Army and their involvement in voluntary social work arises from this. Thus a better understanding of the dynamics of the volunteer organisation should offer considerable insights into volunteering.

Unlike volunteer organisations, mutual aid associations have recently attracted research attention, but more in the USA than in this country. [4] They too embrace a considerable variety, from the 'anonymous' organisations for people with addictions or mental problems, through pensioners' clubs to interest-based action groups. It may be that there is not a lot to distinguish some of the pensioners' clubs run by pensioners from those run by volunteers; the activities may be much the same, as may the motives of those who run the organisation. However, it seems that some of the organisations within this category do help their members in ways which other kinds of organisations cannot, through the sharing of problems and the overcoming of stigma and through reinforcing the informal care provided by families. Mutual aid associations are also significant in a democratic society as being a medium for the expression of consumers' views; and in so far as they seek to carry out a representative function they have a legitimacy not possessed by other kinds of voluntary organisation.

For special agencies and funded charities organisational problems arise not so much from the mobilising of individuals to carry out their work, but in acquiring financial resources. Funded charities usually depend on raising money from a considerable number of donors, and thus on sustaining the support of an extensive network of fund-raisers and donors. These are usually attracted by the appealing nature of the cause the organisation exists to serve, rather than by a close understanding of the work that the organisation is doing. This suggests a number of hypotheses about the factors influencing the development of such organisations. It is essential for them to sustain the right public image, but this is not closely dependent upon, and indeed may be impaired by, keeping up with the latest developments in professional practice; nor are they necessarily under pressures to respond to the work of other agencies. This means that within the broad limits set by the Charity Commission, funded charities have a wide measure of independence. But the opposite side of the same coin is indicated by asking what incentive they have to make good use of this independence. Change in such organisations is particularly likely to be a product of internal dynamics, rather than external forces, and these have been little examined.

In contrast, a special agency has to convince only a small number of officials and politicians that its work deserves support. The main job of the officials and politicians is not to respond to good causes but to carry out their statutory responsibilities. In so doing they will be influenced by whatever public image the organisation may generate, but their more immediate questions are likely to concern how far the statutory authority has an obligation to meet the needs with which the voluntary organisation is concerned, and in so far as it has a responsibility, whether the voluntary organisation is in a better position to do the work than the statutory authority itself. For the voluntary organisation this places a premium on persuading the authority that the needs ought to be met. In some, but not all, circumstances this may point towards enlisting public support through pressure-group activity. The special agency also has to show that whether because of its flexibility, its independence, its low costs or other qualities, it can offer a service which the statutory authority cannot. Relationships between local authorities and the increasing number of special agencies have attracted some attention from political scientists. [5] This is not the place for an excursion into urban politics. These brief points simply serve to suggest that both special agencies and funded charities raise interesting questions that are largely peculiar to those particular categories of organisation.

The different categories of organisation suggested here will be referred to at various points in later chapters, particularly in discussing accountability and relationships with local government in Chapter 6. However, the main point to make in concluding this examination of the varieties of voluntary organisation is that further research, whether it takes the form of case studies or of broader surveys, should not begin with the voluntary sector as a whole but should look in depth at particular types of organisation. It is the dynamics of different kinds of organisation that need to be better understood if judgements are to be made about the potentialities of the sector.

### Notes

1.   K. Newton, *Second City Politics* (Clarendon Press, 1976).

2.   P.F. Cousins, 'Participation and Pluralism in South London', *London Journal*, vol. 4, no. 2 (1978), pp. 204-20.

3.   S. Hatch, *Voluntary Work: a Report of a Survey* (The Volunteer Centre, 1978).

4.   See, for example, A.H. Katz and E.I. Bender (eds.), *The Strength in Us* (New Viewpoints, 1976); G. Caplan and M. Killilea (eds.), *Support Systems and*

*Mutual Help* (Grune Stratton, 1976); and for Britain, D. Robinson and S. Henry, *Self-help and Health* (Martin Robertson, 1977).

    5.   In particular, Newton, *Second City Politics;* J. Dearlove, *The Politics of Policy in Local Government* (Cambridge University Press, 1973); and P.F. Cousins, 'Voluntary Organisations and Local Government in Three South London Boroughs', *Public Administration,* vol. 54 (Spring 1976).

# 4 GROWTH AND CHANGE

Although the history of a few existing voluntary organisations in the three towns goes back to the last century, a majority of them have come into being since 1960. Since the main source of evidence for this study is existing organisations, discussion of the development of the voluntary sector risks being biased very strongly towards the recent past unless additional material can be taken into account. Histories of the voluntary sector in each of the three towns would have been major studies in their own right, requiring an extensive search through local archives even to piece together an incomplete picture. Historical research on these lines was outside the scope of the work reported here. Fortunately, there is a group of studies which does serve to place the results of the present research in perspective. These will be reviewed first, before turning to the evidence about change derived from the research in the three towns.

The first of the studies of other towns, by Stephen Yeo, [1] portrays Reading at the turn of the century, the period of the advent of state collectivism, of popular national news and entertainment media and of the other appurtenances of a mass society. The author describes a world of strong local involvements intertwined with organised religion and suffused with a spirit of self-help and self-improvement. Apart from provision established under the Poor Law, such social services as existed were carried on by voluntary organisations. But only a very few of those organisations and commitments have survived; the world of our grandfathers has been supplanted by a much more extensive range of statutory services that operate within a national rather than an essentially local framework.

## The Voluntary Sector in the 1940s

The course of change is made evident by three reports which appeared midway between the period studied by Yeo and the present. Whatever the strengths of self-supporting local communities, by 1940 it was clear that an adequate framework of social services could only be supplied by the state. During the 1940s, therefore, when the welfare state was in the process of formation, considerable thought was given to the role that the voluntary sector might occupy in the new situation. This concern found expression in three studies. The most well known was Lord Beveridge's *Voluntary Action*, [2] with its companion volume *The Evidence for Voluntary Action*. [3] This was what Beveridge described as his Third Report, following on from *Social Insurance and Allied Services* and *Full Employment in a Free Society*. In addition, a book edited by Bourdillon [4] emerged from the Nuffield College Social Reconstruction Survey and another on not dissimilar lines from the work of Henry Mess. [5] All these present a picture of the voluntary sector as it had developed up to the introduction of the welfare state. Thus they provide an invaluable backcloth for the discussion of more recent developments in the three towns being considered here.

The organisation of Beveridge's report followed his distinction between two main motives inspiring voluntary action — mutual aid and philanthropy. The most numerous category of mutual aid organisations was the friendly societies, which until the development of statutory schemes culminating in the National Insurance Act of 1946 were the main vehicle for insurance against sickness, death and old age. The other expressions of mutual aid noted by Beveridge were the trade unions, building societies, working men's clubs and consumer co-operative societies. As G.D.H. Cole pointed out in the Nuffield study, [6] with the exception of the social insurance carried on by both the friendly societies and trade unions, there was not much of an organised mutual aid element in the social services as they developed over the first half of the century. A significant amount of welfare and advisory work was carried on by trade unions and the co-operative societies made a contribution to social welfare

through educational activities and the work of the Women's
Co-operative Guilds. However, the main thrust of mutual aid
was directed at economic rather than social welfare.

The character of the voluntary social services at this time
is conveyed in a manner most easily compared with the
present study in an account of Burnley by M.P. Hall in the
Nuffield volume. [7] She grouped the work of voluntary
organisations under eight headings. The first of these was
'general social case work'. Burnley did not have strong or co-
ordinated arrangements for case work: instead a number of
different bodies provided relief for those in financial distress.
More typical evidently of towns as large as or larger than
Burnley would have been a centralised case-work agency
offering relief on the lines of the Charity Organisation
Society. The second heading was 'the care of the physically
and mentally handicapped'. There were three main
organisations in this field, one for the blind, one for the deaf,
and one for the mentally handicapped. The first two offered
case work, specialist instruction and social activities, while
mental welfare activities consisted of occupational centres for
the younger defectives. In addition, there was a Cripple
Children's Aid Society, but no equivalent for the adult
handicapped. 'Moral welfare work' was carried out by one of
the oldest welfare organisations in the town, which ran a
home for women and girls in moral danger, and also sought
'to influence public opinion towards the maintenance of a
high standard of sex relationships'. 'Child welfare work' had
been pioneered by voluntary organisations, but subsequently
both the clinic and the nurseries for the children of working
women had been taken over by statutory authorities, leaving
the voluntary organisations in 1943 with only a residual role.
In 'the service of youth', the voluntary sector occupied a
much larger role, despite the recent establishment of youth
centres by the local education authority. Ranging from
Scouts and Guides through numerous church-related clubs
to pre-service organisations like the Sea Cadets and a
substantial youth centre, the voluntary contribution
remained extensive and varied. The work of voluntary
organisations for 'the welfare of the aged' consisted of
running a residential home and a day centre established by
the newly formed Old People's Welfare Committee. The war

had brought a number of special problems, the main one
peculiar to Burnley being the presence of evacuees from the
Channel Islands. One response to this was the establishment
of the Burnley and District Channel Islands Society through
which a club-room was secured. Other responses to the war
not peculiar to Burnley were the formation of a Citizens'
Advice Bureau and the Women's Voluntary Service.
The last of Hall's headings was 'educational work and general
community service'. Here the author made mention of the
thriving Worker's Educational Association, the Co-operative
Guilds and the Citizen's Guild. The last mentioned was
founded in 1935 and by 1943 had 28 affiliated organisations
and was developing towards a council of social service, as well
as being the parent body of the Citizens' Advice Bureau.

In terms of resources, as well as a volume of voluntary help
that could not be quantified, provided mainly by married
women of the middle class, the number of full-time
employees of voluntary organisations amounted to eight.
Apart from youth organisations supported through the Youth
Committee, seven organisations received financial support
from local authorities. In comparison with what one would
expect to find from a contemporary survey, there were fewer
organisations, and the voluntary sector seems to have been
essentially a vehicle for the better-off to help the less
fortunate.

Was this also true of the three towns with which this report
is concerned? A comparison of the situation at the end of the
war with the present depends on two sources of information
— data about the date of formation of existing organisations
in the three towns and inferences from the national surveys
written in the 1940s cited above. The former source does not
cover organisations that have disappeared, whether because of
absorption into the statutory sector or simply through loss of
support. In addition there may have been organisations
operating at a county level meeting some of the needs in the
three towns. Lack of information about these could imply
the complete absence of voluntary provision, when in fact it
was only local provision that was absent. This applies to the
situation in Burnley described above. Despite these severe
limitations, it may help to clarify the pattern of subsequent
development if an attempt is made to sketch the extent of

the voluntary sector in the three towns at the end of the war. The headings used in the analysis that follows are taken from Table 3.1.

*Handicapped and Disabled.* By 1945 specialist organisations for the blind and the deaf were long established and there was some general provision for 'cripples' and 'imbeciles'. These organisations tended to receive financial support from local authorities. Apart from some help for the tubercular there were none of the present specialised organisations catering for people with specific handicaps and diseases.

*Mental Health.* There is no evidence of any voluntary provision organised at the level of the three towns for mental illness as opposed to mental handicap.

*Elderly.* In 1945 old people's welfare councils had recently or were about to come into existence. This evidence of increasing concern for the elderly had also found expression in the formation of a few clubs and centres for pensioners.

*Families and Children.* Moral welfare work under religious auspices was well established, but play was not the object of either voluntary or statutory encouragement. The NSPCC was active in each of the towns, and in two of them there was a children's home, one Catholic and the other part of the National Children's Home.

*Counselling, Rights, Advice.* Voluntary provision was limited to the CABs that came into existence at the beginning of the war.

*Education and Youth.* With Scouts, Guides, Boys' Brigade and numbers of voluntary youth clubs (a few with local authority grants and paid staff) provision in this field was nearer to the present pattern than in any other field. The WEA was also thriving at this time.

*Health and Safety.* The Red Cross and St John's were flourishing, having made an active contribution to the war effort. The voluntary hospitals were about to become part of the new National Health Service.

*Housing.* By the war a number of tenants and/or community associations had come into existence on new estates. Organisations of this kind can be short-lived, and in the three towns there is evidence of only one association in Forgeham surviving from this time. Mention should also be made of the almshouses provided by charities usually of ancient origin.

*Environment.* One local conservation society in
Anglebridge claims to have started in 1940. This and rambling
clubs in two of the towns are evidence of the antecedents of
the present enthusiasm for amenity and environment.

*General Voluntary Effort.* The Women's Voluntary
Service played an important part in the war, and by
redirecting its energies afterwards it has continued to have a
significant role. There are a number of other organisations
animated by a somewhat similar spirit of service that date
from the inter-war years; in each town there are some half
dozen Toc Hs, Rotaries, Soroptimists etc. that existed at this
time. The Salvation Army should also be mentioned under
this heading.

*Other Organisations.* Apart from the one organisation
mentioned under housing, there is no evidence of generalist
neighbourhood organisations surviving from this time. Nor
were there any ethnic organisations.

## Developments since the 1940s

The analysis reported above broadly supports the conclusions
drawn from the writings of the 1940s. There were fewer
organisations and these were nearly all volunteer organisations
rather than mutual aid organisations. Our own survey data
provides evidence about the dates on which organisations
came into existence. This reinforces the impression of much
recent development. Table 4.1 shows that organisations
remaining from the period so far discussed number no more
than some one in five of those presently active. It is also
true that nearly 40 per cent of the organisations surveyed in
1978 had come into existence in the preceding eight years.
At first sight this seems to indicate rapid, even accelerating
growth. But in fact these figures could be compatible with no
growth, or even decline in the number of organisations, if one
were to assume a high level of mortality among voluntary
organisations. Thus it is necessary to know something about
the mortality of organisations before one can say much about
the rate of growth. Many organisations die without a trace,
which makes a retrospective analysis impossible. Fortunately,

**Table 4.1 : The Date of Formation of Voluntary Organisations Existing 1978**

|  | Forgeham | | Anglebridge | | Kirkforth | |
|---|---|---|---|---|---|---|
|  |  | Per |  | Per |  | Per |
|  | No. | cent | No. | cent | No. | cent |
| Before 1914 | 10 | 8 | 3 | 3 | 5 | 6 |
| 1914-45 | 16 | 12 | 12 | 12 | 11 | 14 |
| 1946-60 | 22 | 17 | 18 | 17 | 13 | 16 |
| 1961-70 | 28 | 21 | 30 | 29 | 20 | 25 |
| 1971-78 | 51 | 39 | 36 | 35 | 32 | 40 |
| No information | 5 | 4 | 4 | 4 | — | — |
|  | 132 | 101 | 103 | 100 | 81 | 101 |

Note: No youth clubs, playgroups, parent-teacher associations, pensioners' clubs and tenants' associations are included. See comments in the text.

**Table 4.2 : Changes in the Number of Voluntary Organisations 1975 to 1978**

|  | Forgeham | Anglebridge | Kirkforth | Total |
|---|---|---|---|---|
| Total in 1975/6 | 124 | 97 | 72 | 293 |
| Born | 19 | 13 | 16 | 48 |
| Died | 11 | 7 | 7 | 25 |
| Total in 1977/8 | 132 | 103 | 81 | 316 |
| Percentage increase in 2½ years | 6 | 6 | 13 | 8 |

Note: Youth clubs, pensioners' clubs, playgroups, parent-teacher associations and tenants' associations excluded.

however, the study of the three towns was carried out in two stages separated by an interval of two and a half years. The main aim of the second survey was to record changes in the number of organisations. The resulting data is conveyed in Table 4.2.

Two significant points emerge from the table. The number

of organisations disappearing, or the mortality rate, in each
town amounted to nearly 10 per cent over the two and a half
years, or between 3 and 4 per cent per annum. But the
number of new organisations being formed was distinctly
greater, so that the net growth rate, while higher in Kirkforth
than in the other two towns, averaged some 2.5 per cent per
annum. Taken one year at a time, the rate of change is not
particularly impressive. However, if continued over a longer
period, the change would be substantial. And the high
proportion of existing organisations formed since 1970 does
suggest that the growth recorded between 1975 and 1978
was similar to that occurring since 1970, if not necessarily in
earlier periods. Here therefore is evidence not of any dying
away with the extension of statutory services, but of
substantial and sustained growth in the voluntary sector.

Before taking the discussion a stage further, it should be
noted that the evidence about births and deaths presented in
Tables 4.1 and 4.2 does not cover all the organisations
reported on in Chapter 2. How, therefore, would the inclusion
of the missing organisations alter the picture presented above?
Adequate data was not collected from each town about
youth clubs, pensioners' clubs, playgroups, parent-teacher
associations and tenants' associations. These are the most
widespread and local of voluntary organisations, and though
the data available about them are inadequate for presentation
in tabular form that is not a reason for ignoring them. A few
of the youth and pensioners' clubs date from before 1945,
and a good many more from the immediate post-war period,
with a continuing formation of new organisations since then.
Playgroups, on the other hand, were an innovation of the
1960s, and thus all of them are of recent origin. In the last
year or two the expansion of nursery education has in many
areas curtailed the growth of playgroups, but this in turn has
led to the development of mother and toddler groups which
cater for younger children. In Forgeham, for example,
between 1976 and 1978 there was a decline in the number of
playgroups from 65 to 58, a figure that was more than
counter-balanced by the formation of 12 new mother and
toddler groups. Tenants' associations are another category of
organisation that had its origins in the inter-war years, and
unlike pensioners' and youth clubs their period of rapid

growth seems to have been very recent. The last of the group of organisations omitted from the tables above are parent-teacher associations. These too seem to be a post-war development. The Plowden Report [8] suggested that 17 per cent of primary schools had a PTA in 1963, and one would suspect that the number has grown since then. Summarising this evidence, it would appear that these widespread local organisations have been growing in number no less fast than those that were counted in Tables 4.1 and 4.2. If anything, the effect of their inclusion would be to raise the rates of both births and deaths, the former probably more than the latter.

Another consideration is the possibility that the increase in the total number of organisations could be the result of fragmentation, of more but smaller organisations. To check on this, the organisations in existence in both 1975 and 1978 were asked whether their pattern and level of activities had changed in the two and a half years. In making judgements about whether the changes reported indicated growth or decline the evidence was interpreted cautiously; changes in membership of less than 5 per cent were ignored and movements in opposite directions of membership and activities were interpreted as neutralising each other. The results are presented in Table 4.3.

**Table 4.3 : Change in Organisations Contacted in Both 1975 and 1978**

|                            | Anglebridge | Kirkforth |
|----------------------------|:-----------:|:---------:|
| Activities and membership: |             |           |
| Up                         | 38          | 21        |
| About the same             | 41          | 59        |
| Down                       | 8           | 15        |
| Total                      | 87          | 95        |

The data from the first stage of the Forgeham survey were too sparse to justify tabulation, though the answers that were

obtained had a distribution similar to those from Anglebridge,
where reports of growth easily outweighed reports of decline.
In Kirkforth there was a more even balance, though it is
interesting to remember that proportionately more new
organisations came into existence there than in the other two
towns. Thus, to summarise the general picture, an increase in
the number of voluntary organisations has been combined
with growth rather than decline in the existing organisations.

**Growth Points**

So far the discussion of developments since 1945 has
concentrated on numbers. It is also necessary to describe the
form change has taken in terms of kinds of organisation. One
way of doing this is to examine the main growth points.

Perhaps the most conspicuous is the development of
*organisations for people with specific handicaps or diseases.*
In Forgeham, where there is more emphasis on local social
clubs for the elderly disabled, there are relatively fewer of
them. It is in Anglebridge that the formation of local
branches of specialised national organisations seems to have
gone furthest; this town thus provides an impressive
illustration of developments in this field, which can be
conveyed by a list in order of formation of all the relevant
organisations:

British Limbless Ex-Servicemen's Association (1945)
Social Club for the Blind (1952)
Social Club for the Deaf (1954)
Association for the Physically Handicapped (1955)
St Raphael Club (for the physically handicapped, 1955)
Ileostomy Association (1956)
Multiple Sclerosis Society (1956)
Social Club for the Blind (a second one, 1963)
Association for Spina Bifida and Hydrocephalus (1964)
Physically Handicapped Social Club (for the elderly, 1964)
Physically Handicapped Swimming (1965)
PHAB (physically handicapped able-bodied youth club,
1967)
Spastics Society (1967)

Girl Guides' Extension Branch (1960s)
Disabled Drivers' Association (1968)
Arthritis and Rheumatism Research Council (1968)
Physically Handicapped Riding Group (1969)
Disablement Income Group (1970)
Catholic Handicapped Fellowship (1972)
Deaf Children's Society (1973)
Cystic Fibrosis Research Trust (1974)
Asthma Research Council (1975)
Talking Newspaper (1975)
Epilepsy Action Group (1975)
Physically Handicapped Sports (1975)
Hospital Parents' Association (1976)
National Society for Cancer Relief (1976)
Partially Sighted Society (1977)
Diabetic Association (1978)

The basis of existing organisations on which this growth took place was slender, being limited to national, regional or county bodies for the welfare of the blind, the deaf, the handicapped generally and of sufferers from one or two specific diseases such as tuberculosis. Between our two surveys a long-established Hard of Hearing Social Club came to an end, while short-lived attempts to establish a Crack group for the younger sufferers from multiple sclerosis and musical activities for the physically handicapped proved unfruitful. Anglebridge is a prosperous middle-class area with a rapidly growing population, no doubt particularly conducive to the formation of organisations; and some of the organisations owe their origin to the active part played by the Association for the Physically Handicapped, which is the umbrella body. None of this, however, detracts from the great number and variety of organisations for the handicapped which have come into existence there and to a somewhat lesser degree in the other two towns.

A second point of growth is the *playgroup movement*. The Pre-school Playgroups Association started in 1960, like a number of other voluntary organisations, with a letter to the *Guardian*. Since then playgroups have grown into a widespread national phenomenon. In each of the three towns the number of individual playgroups in relation to the

number of children aged three and four amounted to
between six and eight per thousand. With the extension of
nursery classes for four-year-olds, the movement is now
turning its attention to children below the age of three for
whom mother and toddler groups rather than playgroups as
such are the main vehicle. Although, as explained in Chapter
2, on a strict definition some playgroups count as private
enterprises rather than voluntary organisations, it is difficult
to separate them into distinct categories; taking them
together, the playgroups must represent the largest single
addition since 1960 to the number of organisations included
in this study.

Before leaving the topic of parental involvement, mention
should be made of parent-teacher associations. The scant
attention devoted to them in the research limits what can be
said here. However, it is clear that they represent a significant
post-war addition to the number of voluntary organisations,
though a smaller one than the playgroups.

A third major field of voluntary organisation growth is in
organisations that can be grouped together under the heading
*advice and counselling*. The Citizens' Advice Bureaux which
originated just before the war have experienced a steady
growth in the number of advice-seekers. In addition, a
number of organisations with less general functions have come
into existence. First among these in terms of date is the
Marriage Guidance Council, a branch of which was set up in
the 1950s or early 1960s in each of the three towns. A few
years later came the Samaritans, with subsequently in two of
the towns a Friends of the Samaritans, primarily concerned
with fund-raising. In addition, there are a number of more
local agencies. These were most prominent in Forgeham,
where two neighbourhood general advice centres, a centre
for Asians and a centre primarily for black youth were
established in the 1970s; in addition the Crypt mentioned in
the last chapter has since the 1960s been giving help to
growing numbers seeking advice, mainly but not exclusively
young people. In Anglebridge mention should be made of the
Pastoral Foundation established under Anglican auspices and
offering courses to any who, whether in a voluntary or a
statutory capacity, wish to acquire skills in counselling. This
was attracting growing interest from a wide field. Kirkforth

witnessed a short-lived rights and information centre which took a more radical stance than the CAB, and recently the formation of a branch of Cruse that was aiming to provide counselling for widows. Developments in advice-giving are significant not so much for the number of new organisations involved, but for the predominant part played by voluntary organisations in the emergence of a new set of services.

Another growth point is *neighbourhood organisations*. In some senses the playgroups already discussed and many of the clubs for young people and pensioners are neighbourhood organisations. However, the ones of interest here are those with a more general approach. The most general are the community associations. Forgeham had 14, some dating from the 1970s and others from around 1950. In Anglebridge there were 4, none more than ten years old, while in Kirkforth there is a single community centre. The 4 residents' associations in Anglebridge should also be mentioned, as should the 31 tenants' associations in Forgeham, most of recent origin. Forgeham's tenants' associations were something of a shadow army, but a few had a substantial existence and concerned themselves with more than tenants' grievances. Their absence from the other two towns at any rate in part reflects the fact that the incidence of tenants' associations is closely related to the size of a local authority's housing stock. [9] A final group of organisations that deserves inclusion here are neighbourhood or community care schemes: these are primarily concerned with the elderly and have been coming into existence all over the country. In Anglebridge there were 3 and in Forgeham 5, all of recent origin. All told this is a disparate set of organisations, but it does seem to signify a growing readiness for people to act together at the neighbourhood level.

Three other growth points should also be noted – *special need housing, ethnic organisations* and *environmental organisations*. The longest-standing of the voluntary housing projects in Anglebridge and Kirkforth is the Abbeyfield Society, which since the early 1960s has been using a converted house to provide sheltered accommodation for the elderly. In Forgeham a local Abbeyfield has only just been founded; the longest-lived project in the town was a hostel for vagrants started in 1958. Forgeham has a relatively large number of vagrants, and a second hostel, run by a religious order, was established there in 1972. Other recent projects are a Harrambee hostel for black youth, hostels for homeless young people run by the Crypt and hostels for former mental patients. In the other two towns the need for occasional temporary accommodation was being met by a shelter run by volunteers. Beyond this, the Abbey Trust founded in 1973 and described in Chapter 3 had expanded quickly in reponse to the needs of homeless and rootless people, particularly addicts and ex-prisoners.

The ethnic and environmental organisations require no further comment here except to say that nearly all the former and about half the latter have come into existence in the past decade.

The pinpointing of a limited number of growth points should not convey the impression that since the 1940s little development has occurred elsewhere. The WRVS in all three towns and the Red Cross in two have continued to mobilise a substantial number of volunteers, while Hospital Friends have come to play an established part in support of the health service. In each town there has come into existence a branch of the Society for Mentally Handicapped Children, though Forgeham is alone in having an Association for Mental Health, dating from 1971. Branches of Alcoholics Anonymous have been formed in each town while, again only in Forgeham, there is a recently established Gamblers Anonymous.

Altogether it might seem that to describe the growth of the voluntary sector is to chronicle the social concerns of our times. But this is not the whole of the picture. There are some fields where the voluntary sector has played little part and others where it has declined. PTAs apart, the schools are one of these fields. In Kirkforth a free school was born and died in the period between our two surveys, while the local affiliate of the Campaign for the Advancement of State Education declined. In Anglebridge it faded out altogether, while in Forgeham there never was a CASE group; but the National Campaign for Nursery Education also faded out, while the National Association for Gifted Children seemed inactive.

In family planning the role of the voluntary sector has also declined, but in this case because the state has assumed responsibility. The same is true to a lesser degree of adoption and of services for the blind and the deaf, where in each case the creation of the local authority social services departments has led to a transfer of some services established by voluntary organisations to the state. But with these exceptions the dominant pattern in recent years seems not to have been what is often assumed to be the conventional one — a statutory take-over of services pioneered by the voluntary sector. Rather the state has extended its activities into fields where voluntary organisations have been active more as pressure groups than as providers of services themselves.

## Why the Growth?

This chapter has presented a picture of substantial and sustained growth in the number of voluntary organisations. Evidence about changes in the level of individual participation in voluntary organisations in the three towns is not available. However, recent evidence from the General Household Survey seems to be symptomatic; this reported a rise between 1973 and 1977 from 8.1 per cent to 9.6 per cent in the proportion of people who said they had taken part in voluntary social work in the preceding month. [10] It might have been expected that as the statutory sector expanded, the voluntary sector would have become less necessary and thus declined. On this line of reasoning the growth of the voluntary sector since 1975 could be explained by the recent cut-backs in public expenditure. But the growth seems to go back considerably further than that, to a time when it coincided with a rapid expansion of statutory services. Thus the two sectors cannot be interpreted as essentially replacements for each other. How, therefore, can the growth of the voluntary sector be explained?

Some changes in the voluntary sector can be attributed to particular factors. Thus the population of Anglebridge has been growing fast, and this alone must have generated new organisations. More specifically, the Association for Spina Bifida and Hydrocephalus has come into existence as a result of developments in medical practice which led to the survival of more children with spina bifida. But such explanations do not account for the overall growth. Further light on factors leading to the formation of voluntary organisations is shed by an analysis of how new organisations came into existence, of how they were actually triggered off.

This is a topic on which we were able to collect some information when inquiring about organisations formed between the two stages of the survey. The information obtained was not at all detailed and related only to 58 organisations, but it does convey something about the process. The source of the impetus can be divided into six distinct categories. Occasionally there was an overlap when different parties were involved, but in most cases the simplified account conveyed to us suggests an uncomplicated process.

The type of trigger to which the creation of the largest number of organisations can be attributed (16) are the staff of statutory agencies acting in an official or semi-official capacity. For example, a teacher in a special school was the impulse behind the formation of a deaf children's society; a medical social worker initiated a group for the parents of handicapped children: and in what was a more elaborate exercise a number of professionals round a community health council were seeking the funds to set up a hospice for cancer sufferers. Sometimes, as with neighbourhood care groups in Anglebridge, it was part of the professionals' duties to engage in this kind of activity; in other situations the individuals concerned were taking an initiative somewhat beyond but related to their formal brief.

Another source of a number of new organisations (9) was either a single individual or a group with a problem coming forward to bring together others who shared the problem. Thus it was the parent of a child with diabetes who promoted a public meeting which led to the establishment of a local branch of the Diabetic Society. A further example is the recently disabled social worker who brought into being the Disabled Action Group discussed in Chapter 3, while a third example is a group of residents on a new private estate who, facing problems with the contractor, set up a residents' association. Organisations formed in this way are ones operating on a mutual aid basis. They have their counterpart in individuals or groups animated by a philanthropic motive.

Thus a branch of the Howard League for Penal Reform was established by two prison visitors who wanted to create a forum in which they could discuss the kind of issues arising from their work as prison visitors. This also seemed to be the impetus behind one of the new neighbourhood care organisations, where, rather than being the primary initiator, the SSD quickly came in to give support. Another example of this kind of impetus is a group animated by a cause, like that leading to the formation of a local Friends of the Earth. Eight organisations owed their existence to individuals acting on this philanthropic basis. Closely related, in some senses a subsection of the previous category, are initiatives taken by churches. Ten new organisations were attributable to initiatives from this source, mostly clubs for young people or pensioners, but also in one case a workshop for the elderly in new, community-orientated church premises.

The fifth distinct category of initiatives are those which represent an outgrowth of existing voluntary organisations. Sometimes, as with the formation of a local branch of Cruse, this was an expression of deliberate, developmental activity by a national organisation seeking to inaugurate new local branches. In other instances an existing local organisation separated out a distinct set of its activities. This was what happened with the establishment of a Friends of the Samaritans alongside a local Samaritans. Eight of the new organisations seemed to come into this category. Finally, there were 7 new organisations which could not be so clearly classified; these were mostly the product of joint activities, as between a local Pre-school Playgroups Association and an SSD playgroup organiser in establishing a new playgroup, or joint activity by the SSD and the Community Relations Council in promoting a project for Asian youth.

Reviewing these triggering activities as part of a more general developmental process, 25 organisations seemed to have come into existence as a result of deliberate action by the personnel of statutory agencies or existing voluntary organisations. Only 15 were the product of individuals acting spontaneously; while the 10 church-sponsored organisations perhaps occupy an intermediate position between deliberate intervention and spontaneous community initiatives. What seems significant is the prominence of deliberate intervention in stimulating the development of voluntary organisations.

Thus an important factor in explaining the growth of voluntary organisations was deliberate encouragement. In recent years it has been government policy to promote voluntary action. At the national level this has found expression in the formation of the Voluntary Services Unit, and at local level SSDs and hospitals have created numbers of posts with the objective of encouraging voluntary work and voluntary organisations. But in order for public policy to have an impact there must have been a disposition towards participation in voluntary activity.

In comparison with earlier periods, the impetus behind the development of the voluntary sector has changed significantly. As already noted, the impulse towards mutual aid found little expression in the social services before the war; development characteristically followed in the wake of the crusading philanthropists, the Dr Barnardo or the Octavia Hill. Crusading philanthropists have not disappeared; how else would, for example, Chad Varah or Erin Pizzey be classified? And the philanthropic motive, to follow Beveridge's terminology, is still the main force behind the established organisations that mobilise a large amount of voluntary help like the WRVS and the Scouts, as well as of newer developments like neighbourhood care schemes, the advice services and the direct recruitment of volunteers by statutory services.

Characteristic of much contemporary development, however, is the letter or feature in a women's magazine or a women's page which elicits an immediate response from many others experiencing the same situation as the writer, out of which a new organisation is brought into being. It is this kind of impulse that has animated much of the growth described in this chapter. Thus a majority of the local organisations for the handicapped, the playgroups and the tenants' associations and most of the other neighbourhood organisations are people acting and campaigning for themselves and their families rather than on behalf of others whose situation is essentially different from their own.

All this is partly a consumers' movement, on a par with that existing in other fields, and a reaction to the extension of and greater dependence on statutory services. However, it does not seem to be essentially, let alone exclusively, protective in character. Putting it in very general terms, the demand for and expectations of public services have been growing. Indeed the development of society seems to generate a constant stream of needs, the meeting of which requires organised rather than informal action. These are not all within the capabilities of statutory action, and instead of simply leaving provision to the state, increasing numbers of people have been seeking an active part in the giving of services and in influencing their development.

## Notes

1.   S. Yeo, *Religion and Voluntary Organisations in Crisis* (Croom Helm, 1976).

2.   Lord Beveridge  *Voluntary Action* (Allen and Unwin, 1948).

3.   Lord Beveridge and A.F. Wells (eds.), *The Evidence for Voluntary Action* (Allen and Unwin, 1949).

4.   A.F.C. Bourdillon (ed.), *Voluntary Social Services* (Methuen, 1945).

5.   H.A. Mess, *Voluntary Social Services since 1918*  (Kegan Paul, Trench and Trubner, 1948).

6.   G.D.H. Cole, 'Mutual Aid Movements in their Relation to Voluntary Social Service' in Bourdillon, *Voluntary Social Services*, pp. 118-34.

7.   M.P. Hall, 'Voluntary Organisations in Burnley' in Bourdillon, *Voluntary Social Services*, pp. 235-62.

8.   *Children and their Primary Schools* (The Plowden Report) (HMSO, 1967).

9.   A. Richardson, 'The Politics of Participation: a Study of Schemes for Tenant Participation in Council Housing Management' (unpublished PhD thesis, London School of Economics, 1977), Chapters 6 and 7.

10.   Office of Population Censuses and Surveys, *General Household Survey 1977* (HMSO), Table 7.8.

# 5 THE ROLE OF THE VOLUNTARY SECTOR

There is still no better argument to be found about the role of voluntary organisations than Chapter 9 of the Webbs' *The Prevention of Destitution*. [1] Written in the wake of the controversy following the Report of the Royal Commission on the Poor Law of 1909, during the early stages of the formation of the welfare state, the Webbs were concerned to demolish the grander pretensions of the voluntary agencies and put forward in their place a role for the voluntary sector compatible with a strong interpretation of the responsibilities of the state. In so doing they distinguished two theories or models about the relationships between the state and the voluntary sector — the parallel bars and the extension ladder.

The parallel bars theory signified a view that voluntary organisations should provide services in parallel to those of the state, but for a different clientele. In relation to the Victorian Poor Law this meant that voluntary agencies should support the respectable and the deserving, to prevent them falling into the workhouse, an institution for deterring the 'undeserving poor'. However, as the Webbs pointed out, the voluntary agencies did not have the resources to help more than a few of the deserving. All sorts of people —

the most deserving aged, the most blameless incurable sick, the chronically infirm who have led beautiful lives of patient endurance, the innocent wives and children of thriftless unemployed men, the man or woman broken down by a hard life of excessive toil [therefore had to enter the workhouse along with the] workshys, the drunkards and the wastrels (pp. 232-3).

The Webbs proposed instead the extension ladder theory. This recognised that 'in the United Kingdom of today, voluntary agencies are superior to the public authorities in

three main features; in invention and initiative, in their
ability to lavish unstinted care on particular cases, and in the
intensity and variety of the religious influences that they can
bring to bear on personal character' (p. 240). Nevertheless
they lacked resources and were most unevenly distributed;
thus they could not provide universal services, nor did they
have any powers of enforcement. Hence the Webbs advanced
the concept:

> Not of 'parallel bars' wholly separate and distinct from
> each other, with a large intervening space of 'missed cases';
> but of an 'extension ladder' placed firmly on the
> foundation of an enforced minimum standard of life, but
> carrying onward the work of the Public Authorities to far
> finer shades of physical, moral and spiritual perfection
> (p. 252).

The Webbs' view of the role of voluntary organisations was
based on what they took to be the inherent strengths and
weaknesses of the voluntary and statutory sectors. Beveridge,
in his *Voluntary Action* [2] written  nearly forty years later,
adopted a broader more philosophical view:

> In a totalitarian society all action outside the citizen's
> home, and it may be much that goes on there, is directed
> or controlled by the State. By contrast, the vigour and
> abundance of Voluntary Action outside one's home,
> individually and in association with other citizens, for
> bettering one's own life and that of one's fellows, are the
> distinguishing marks of a free society (p. 10).

While equally:

> The business motive, in the field covered by this Report
> is seen in continual or repeated conflict with the
> Philanthropic Motive, and has too often been successful . . .
> The business motive is a good servant but a bad master,
> and a society which gives itself up to the dominance of the
> business motive is a bad society (p. 322).

Thus Beveridge advocated state encouragement of voluntary

action primarily because he favoured a plural society imbued with the spirit of mutual aid and philanthropy, rather than because there were some things voluntary organisations could do better than statutory agencies. He did not use the words 'participation' or 'involvement', which have become so much a part of the modern vocabulary. But they did find a place in the Wolfenden Report which sought to apply a similar pluralistic philosophy to the conditions of the 1970s.

These are broad brush analyses of the part played by statutory and voluntary sectors. But it is difficult to say how far they remain applicable in the present situation without a closer analysis of what is actually being done in different fields. This in turn requires a set of more detailed distinctions with which to examine the work of particular organisations. Thus the discussion that follows is devoted first to clarifying the different kinds of roles of voluntary organisations. Then in the main body of the chapter these are applied to the various fields of provision, followed by some evidence of consumers' views. Finally, the argument returns to the broad issues raised by Beveridge and the Webbs, and a new distinction is suggested which seeks to encapsulate the alternatives for the voluntary sector in an era of greatly extended statutory provision.

## The Role of Voluntary Organisations: Some Distinctions

In relation to the statutory sector a lot of what the voluntary sector does can be placed under two headings — extending provision and improving the quality of statutory provision. Extensions can take various forms. One form of extension is 'more of the same'. For example, many of the benevolent funds and small local charities provide grants for people in 'necessitous circumstances'. The extra money is not different from what the recipient obtains by way of a state pension or supplementary benefits. Most extensions, however, are different from statutory provision, and can be divided into services which are in some places provided by the state or could be if the resources were available, and those which lie outside the capabilities of statutory agencies. Talking newspapers for the blind exemplify the former. These

represent a service recently and widely developed by
voluntary organisations which is not available from the state.
However, it is easy to conceive of the state taking
responsibility for this service if it decided to allocate the
necessary resources. In other situations, voluntary
organisations provide a service which the state could not
provide nearly as well, or would not be able to provide at all,
even if it did have the resources. This seems to be true of
neighbourly visiting, befriending and the kind of mutual
support people gain through organisations like Alcoholics
Anonymous.

The most obvious way in which voluntary organisations
bring about improvements in statutory provision is by acting
as pressure groups. This critical role is a widely recognised
one for voluntary organisations, but not the only source of
improvement. The provision of independent advice and
information to consumers of statutory services can have a
similar effect, as can the introduction of volunteers into
residential institutions. More generally, the pioneering
activities of voluntary organisations and the way they act as
a medium for community involvement can be seen as
beneficial for the statutory sector.

It would be a mistake to imply that all voluntary action
can be divided into that which extends and that which
improves, since much of it does both. For example, voluntary
organisations that provide residential care for children and
the elderly add to the total quantity of what is available, and
in so doing both widen its variety and give the consumers of
residential care (or those acting on their behalf) a choice.
Thus they extend provision and by creating diversity and
alternatives they may at the same time exert improving
influences on statutory services. Pioneering services are in a
similar position. *Ipso facto* they extend provision, and in so
far as the innovation is successfully adopted by the state,
they bring about improvements.

In relation to informal sources of care both voluntary and
statutory services may act in three ways — as replacements,
as reliefs or as reinforcements. Although the extent and
significance of informal care is receiving increasing
recognition, there is as yet remarkably little well substantiated
evidence about the actual impact of voluntary and statutory

provision on it. This needs to be better understood, if only to
test the proposition that encouragement of informal care is
no more than a way of increasing the domestic responsibilities
of women. However, for the present purpose of clarifying the
distinction between the three roles some brief illustrations
may suffice. Long-term residential care takes those receiving
it largely out of the orbit of informal care, and thus replaces
it. Day care and short-stay residential care, on the other hand,
temporarily reduce the responsibilities carried by informal
carers, and thus may be interpreted as reliefs. Financial help,
aids and adaptations to the home and psychological support
neither replace nor relieve, but rather reinforce informal care.
These three roles can be played by both voluntary and
statutory services, but the participatory character of many
voluntary organisations, particularly the mutual aid groups,
gives the voluntary sector certain advantages in taking on a
reinforcing role.

Before making any more general statements about the
role of voluntary organisations further examination of what
they do is needed. This will both test the validity of these
distinctions and in so far as they are valid, clarify the parts
voluntary organisations actually play. Residential, day and
domiciliary care in the personal social services field will be
considered in turn, followed by counselling and advice, health,
education and the environment.

## Residential Care

As far as residential care is concerned, national data [3]
indicate that voluntary organisations provide approximately
one in ten of the places for children in residential care
(though this figure is declining) and about one in six of the
places in homes for the elderly. In Anglebridge there were no
voluntary homes for children or old people, but Kirkforth
had a Catholic home for children and for old people and
Forgeham contained a branch of the National Children's
Homes, a hostel for adolescents and two voluntary homes for
old people. The charges for most of the residents in these
homes were paid by local authorities. These voluntary
organisations were not providing services fundamentally

different from the equivalent local authority homes; but they represent an addition to the total number of places available, and an element of variety and choice relevant to those with religious affiliations. In addition, there are a small number of 'Friends' organisations which both raise small sums of money for additional facilities in statutory homes and visit the residents there. But this sort of complementary/additional function for voluntary organisations is only very weakly developed in the three towns.

Another less well established form of residential care is that provided for those usually described as 'the single homeless'. These may be vagrants or those requiring short-stay accommodation in an emergency; others like alcoholics, drug addicts, ex-mental patients and ex-offenders need a supportive environment over a longer period. A further category are the homeless families, including battered wives and their children. Apart from a number of hostels run by the Supplementary Benefits Commission and the local authority homeless families accommodation, statutory provision to meet these needs is very limited. Certainly there was none in the three towns studied. Instead this field was marked by the many pioneering voluntary projects mentioned in Chapters 3 and 4.

In meeting these needs the voluntary agencies were both pioneers and the sole providers. Whether they will remain the sole providers remains to be seen; the people they help represent unpopular causes and for this reason the local authorities may continue to support voluntary organisations rather than enter the field directly themselves. In addition, some of these voluntary organisations are vehicles for the practical expression of strong personal commitments, Christian in the case of the Abbey Trust and the two Forgeham homes for down-and-outs, and more ideological and political in the case of the women's refuges. The regimes that result from this commitment can hardly be reproduced in a statutory setting, and statutory equivalents could also cost considerably more. [4] Beyond this some of the voluntary organisations also act as pressure groups, aiming to secure public recognition for the needs they are seeking to meet, particularly in the form of funding for their own organisation, but also through changes in local authority policies regarding the allocation of their own housing stock.

**Domiciliary and Day Care**

The services offered by most of the voluntary organisations
active in the personal social services field come under the
heading of domiciliary and day care. Starting with the under-
fives, playgroups make a substantial addition to total
provision, which is also a partial alternative to local authority
day nurseries and nursery classes. Voluntary organisations
like the NSPCC and the church-related family welfare agencies
also offer more specialised services and support for families
with children. Nevertheless the main responsibility for
supporting families lies with the statutory SSDs. The
rationale for the voluntary extensions to these services tends
to lie either in their specialisation and expertise or in the
ability of mutual aid organisations like Gingerbread to offer
support of a different kind.

The great variety of activities for the handicapped are
difficult to summarise. For most of the handicapped the
statutory sector now provides a core of basic services —
health care in the community from GPs and district nurses,
day centres, home helps and various home aids and
adaptations. Much of what the voluntary organisations do
comes into two categories. In so far as they provide services,
they mostly offer something that is additional to statutory
provision. This is true of the regular meetings for social and
recreational activities which constitute the main weekly
function of many organisations, of the special activities like
outings and holidays, as also of the recently developed
sporting and recreational activities for the younger disabled,
like riding and swimming. All these could be provided by the
local authority, though at considerably greater cost. It may
be that some at any rate will in due course be taken on by the
statutory authorities and thereby come to exemplify
successful pioneering by voluntary organisations.

The other major voluntary contribution is less tangible and
has more of a moral and psychological character, stemming
mainly from the participatory nature of the activities. This
theme was the main one emerging from questionnaires
completed for the Wolfenden Committee in answer to a
question about whether voluntary organisations could do a
better job than statutory authorities. The broad theme had

several facets. One stressed the involvement of the handicapped themselves:

> Only an ileostomist can do the visiting as it should be done. As an association we are free of red tape (Anglebridge, Ileostomy).

> The problems which are asociated with a particular-type of disability can only be *really* appreciated by those suffering from like disabilities and membership of BLESMA is only open to those who thus qualify (Kirkforth).

> Yes, because we are voluntary workers for one another (Forgeham Disabled Drivers Association).

Mentioned less often, but a feature particularly of the organisations for handicapped children, was the involvement of the families:

> At the local grass-roots level they are more intimately concerned with the problem of the mentally handicapped child, many of the members have first-hand experience (Kirkforth, Society for Mentally Handicapped Children).

Another important facet was the personal, non-bureaucratic character of voluntary care:

> We are available seven days a week and meet them at church and club, so solve problems before they loom large (Social Club for the Deaf, Anglebridge).

> Government need too much time to make decisions and don't understand compassion. Our organisations is a big understanding family (ASBAH, Forgeham).

> The atmosphere at our day centre is superb. Everyone is free and easy and I think we have a better atmosphere than would exist at a state-run affair (Multiple Sclerosis, Forgeham).

A government agency tends to become concerned with

wages for its staff: top heavy and inefficient: cynical and souless. The voluntary is *concerned* and has *soul* (Fellowship for the Disabled, Forgeham).

Voluntary organisations are usually caring and can be more personal and flexible (Talking Newspaper, Anglebridge).

These of course are the claims made by voluntary organisations. The staff of statutory services would no doubt challenge the view that they are less caring than volunteers, and might argue convincingly that sometimes fellow sufferers or compassionate volunteers may through ignorance or prejudice give the wrong sort of help. Nevertheless, even if the claims are only partially valid, they indicate a distinctive characteristic of voluntary services. As well as being vehicles for the expression of mutual aid and philanthropy, which can be accounted good in themselves, the translation of these motives into action can generate a special sort of support, which is different from rather than simply additional to statutory services and can also link with and reinforce the informal carers.

Any analysis of voluntary organisations for the handicapped needs to recognise a prominent characteristic of many of them − specificity. This can give them an understanding of what it is to be handicapped and a commitment not readily available within the statutory services. Statements to the effect that those with experience of the same problem are best fitted to help reflect this advantage as well as the psychological value of sharing. However, it is at the level of national headquarters rather than the local branch that voluntary organisations tend to be notable for their specialist resources and for expertise of a professional kind.

At the local level most of the organisations for the handicapped worked quite closely with the statutory services. Where they did not do so it seemed in the three towns more a result of statutory neglect than antagonism on the part of the voluntary organisation. Within this kind of relationship the voluntary organisations were able to communicate needs, but seldom did they openly challenge the adequacy of existing provision by taking up an active pressure-group role.

Indeed DIG in Anglebridge and the Disabled Action Group in Forgeham were the only organisations of those studied in this field that acted primarily and explicitly as pressure groups.

The discussion has so far concentrated on organisations for the handicapped. Many of the handicapped are also elderly and the same conclusions can in large measure be drawn for the day and domiciliary care provided by organisations for the elderly. Amongst the most numerous are the pensioners' clubs, which are an expression in different combinations of mutual aid and philanthropy. Mention should also be made of the significant addition to statutory services constituted by the voluntary contribution to the meals on wheels service, and also the development of neighbourhood care schemes which promise to reinforce informal care.

Demographic change is leading to a substantial increase in the number of isolated and/or incapacitated old people. Although they will require many services for which they will have to depend on the statutory authorities, they will also need a lot of practical help with day-to-day tasks, social contact and surveillance. There are obvious attractions in seeking to meet the latter by the reinforcement of informal patterns of care.

## Advice and Counselling

This field represents a major growth point for the voluntary séctor, and one where its predominance raises particularly interesting questions for its relationship with statutory services and their professional staff. The main voluntary organisations which are active in each of the towns are the Citizens' Advice Bureau, the Samaritans and the Marriage Guidance Council. The numbers using these services are large. Thus in the year 1974/5 in Anglebridge the CAB had 9,000 callers, the Samaritans 1,700 new clients and the Marriage Guidance Council reported that it had held nearly 1,800 counselling sessions. And the general picture is one of increasing demand. These three bodies represent the established core of voluntary provision. The other components of it are more varied and were mentioned in Chapters 3 and 4.

On the statutory side there was in each town a town hall

information point. As well as giving information directly, these referred callers on to the relevant local authority department. The libraries too were a source of information, while much of the activity of social workers can be described as advice-giving and counselling. In addition, Forgeham had established a Consumers' Advice Centre.

A proper discussion of the reasons for the growing demand for advice and counselling would be out of place here, though clearly in part it reflects the greater extent and complexity of statutory services and regulations nowadays. What does deserve examination here is the preponderant role of the voluntary sector in this field. Although officials from many local authority departments spend a considerable amount of time relating to and providing information and advice for the public, the organisations that make this their main function are nearly all voluntary. One obvious reason for this is the need for an independent source of advice, not itself part of the service or the problem about which the advice is sought. Similarly in the case of counselling, where the problems are personal and not so much about access to statutory services, an agency like the Samaritans offers confidentiality with no risk that problems will be brought to the attention of 'the authorities' who may want to do something about them. In the words of the Kirkforth branch, 'the service can be used with complete anonymity . . . Perhaps it is fulfilling the role filled in the past by the priest.'

Those who give advice on behalf of the CAB, the Samaritans and the MGC are volunteers. Although they are obliged to go through a selection and training process, they are not full-time professionals. What can be seen as the counselling function or promoting 'the improved functioning of an individual through personal relationships' has been claimed as the core of social work. [5] Yet as Goldberg in particular has pointed out [6] this kind of activity seems nowadays to occupy only a small proportion of the time of social service department social workers. Instead it is being taken on by trained volunteers working for voluntary organisations.

This trend is partly a result of differences in the clientele of the two sorts of service. Survey data [7] about the clients of the Marriage Guidance Council suggest that, though there is a

small bias towards the higher social classes, they reflect
fairly closely the social class composition of the population
as a whole and the age distribution of the divorcing
population. There is as yet no comprehensive data about the
users of the CAB service. However, a survey in three inner
London boroughs [8] suggested that in terms of social class the
users of the CAB corresponded with the whole population,
save only a small tendency for the lower social classes to
make more use of the service. The Samaritans have recently
brought together data about all those who contacted their
branches for the first time in 1976. [9] Males exceeded females
by four to three and those in their twenties seemed to make
proportionately the most use of the service, with a steady
fall-off with increasing age thereafter. Evidence about social
status and occupation was difficult to relate to the population
as a whole because of incomplete data, but it seemed that
the unemployed, the unskilled and, interestingly, also people
in professional jobs were relatively more likely to contact the
Samaritans. It is also relevant to relate the characteristics of
the clients of the Samaritans to the characteristics of those
who do commit suicide. The incidence of suicide is greater
among males than among females in the ratio of
approximately three to two, and in contrast with Samaritan
clients, rises steadily with age. [10] However, the incidence by
age of those who unsuccessfully attempt suicides apparently
diverges less from the age distribution of those who contact
the Samaritans. This is not the place to pursue further the
interesting questions raised by this set of data. Suffice it to
say that the users of all the three main voluntary services
seem to contrast quite sharply with the people on the case-
load of a social services department. Goldberg's research [11]
suggests that with the partial exception of the elderly, the
cases are drawn highly disproportionately from the lower
social classes and from problem housing estates. Thus the
broad picture is one of the main voluntary organisations
catering for the population as a whole, in a manner
comparable to the National Health Service, while the field
social workers of the statutory services tend to deal with the
more deprived. This is a reversal of the voluntary and
statutory roles to be found in, for example, the housing of the
single homeless.

## Health

With the establishment of the National Health Service the voluntary sector in the health field lost the central role it once occupied; and the recent reorganisations of family planning and the ambulance service have led to the assimilation of further voluntary services into the statutory sector. Organisations concerned with the handicapped or with particular diseases like cancer have been discussed in this book mainly under the heading of the personal social services rather than the health services. But in fact these organisations are in varying degrees concerned with health care as well as social care; in some cases the health aspect predominates or cannot be separated from the social aspect. Thus the Ileostomy Association helps those who have undergone ileostomies with both the medical and the social consequences of their condition, while the fund-raising organisations like those for cancer research and the Arthritis and Rheumatism Research Council augment the resources available for research aimed at improving medical care.

The ways in which the voluntary sector contributes to the overall pattern of health care is well illustrated by the Red Cross. In Anglebridge it has over a hundred members and is more active there than in the other two towns. Part of its work consists of helping in the hospitals; there is a rota of volunteers to feed young handicapped children and assist in the X-ray unit, and a beauty care service is provided for long-stay geriatric patients. The hospital trolley service in Anglebridge is run by the WRVS, but outside the hospitals the Red Cross maintains a medical aids loan service, runs a small hobbies club for the housebound elderly, arranges escorts and drivers, organises holidays for handicapped children and operates an ambulance used at public events and for transporting the handicapped. In addition the Red Cross undertakes a considerable amount of training in first aid and also gives instruction in basic nursing to members who when so qualified are known as VADs.

In defining its role in relation to the National Health Service the Red Cross favours the term supplementary; it sees itself as an extension which supports, not an alternative to statutory provision. The work of most of the other voluntary

organisations also comes into this category. The Hospital
Friends raise money for extra facilities; in limited measure
they also mobilise volunteers to help within the hospitals,
though in Kirkforth most of this was being done directly by
the two volunteer organisers employed by the hospital. Some
of these supplementary or additional services, like the beauty
care and the hospital radio, also have a pioneering character
and could be more widely adopted by the statutory services
in due course. However, it would be a mistake to define all of
what the voluntary sector does in the health field as simply
additional or supplementary. Thus the National Childbirth
Trust, which was active in two of the towns, offered guidance
to pregnant women that can be seen as alternative as well as
additional to that available from the statutory services; and
the visiting of people in hospital is significant because visitors
from 'the community' may both offer the long-stay patient
personal contact of a quality not available from within the
institution, and by opening the institution up inhibit the
development of the oppressive practices that can occur in
long-stay hospitals. Nevertheless there was little evidence in
the three towns of voluntary organisations acting as pressure
groups in the health field or of any direct challenge from
them to the health professions.

The role of voluntary organisations in relation to informal
or self-care in health has attracted very little comment. No
doubt, despite the fact that people do in reality carry out a
lot of health care for themselves, this is because health is so
widely assumed to be a matter for the professionals.
However, there was a Weight Watchers group in Anglebridge,
and some of the specialised mutual aid groups, like the
Diabetic Associations recently formed in two of the towns,
were helping sufferers and their families look after themselves
and were thus a means of reinforcing informal care. The role
of the Red Cross and St John's in giving training in first aid
and basic nursing is also significant as a way of disseminating
health knowledge and skills among the population at large.


**Education and Youth**

Education was peripheral to the interests of the Wolfenden

Committee. But since it constitutes one of the five main social services and a significant field for voluntary action, at least a brief discussion of it is required. Education is moreover a field where some of the relationships between the state and the voluntary sector have become so institutionalised as to give a special meaning to the term voluntary. The voluntary contribution can be placed under five headings: parent-teacher associations, youth clubs, voluntary-aided schools, pressure groups and the Workers' Educational Association. The role of the education service in supporting community associations will be considered under the heading of neighbourhood organisations.

As noted in an earlier chapter, PTAs seem to exist in a large minority of LEA schools. They serve to enlist parental support for the school, which may take tangible forms in the provision of additional resources such as a swimming pool. They also act as a channel for involving the parents in the education of the children, which can be seen as a complementary extension to the statutory service. However, they do not necessarily do this, and equally the same kinds of objectives can be pursued without the formal medium of a PTA.

The WEA represents primarily a source of adult education alternative to the provision of university extra-mural departments and the local education authorities. It was active in each of the three towns and has an established place in the pattern of provision, receiving three-quarters of its funds from central and local government. As noted by the Russell Committee, [12] it has a pioneering tradition for developing adult education opportunities for groups not catered for by other providers, and is noted for encouraging the active participation of its members in both the arrangement and the conduct of classes.

PTAs and the WEA are vehicles for community involvement. The Campaign for the Advancement of State Education also performs this function as a by-product of its main pressure-group role. Occurring in only two of the three towns, it seemed to be losing rather than gaining impetus during the period of our inquiries.

The voluntary part of the youth service has recently received more attention than most of the other fields of voluntary activity examined in this book. [13] The youth service as a whole represents a well developed pluralism in the sense that a majority of the provision is made through voluntary channels and established machinery usually exists to link the two sectors. In this respect Anglebridge was untypical on account of the predominance of the statutory sector there. But there and elsewhere young people can choose from a large number of alternatives ranging from the small church clubs, the well known national uniformed organisations like Scouts and Guides and the voluntary clubs with premises of their own to the statutory, school-based youth centres. The voluntary sector is the vehicle for the expression of personal commitment, for fostering the religious and/or ethnic identity of young people or, as in the case of the military and the Red Cross cadets, for introducing them to particular skills and allegiances. All these activities are supported by arrangements at national and local level for the provision of financial and other resources from government.

The voluntary-aided schools were not included in the surveys carried out for the Wolfenden Committee. In each town there was one selective school which had voluntary-aided status, as well as a number of Catholic comprehensives. These schools date from the time when great importance was attached to providing education along denominational lines. Today, by avoiding complete local authority control, they still offer an element of choice in respect of religious affiliations, and in a few areas where a voluntary-aided school has not accepted the selection criteria adopted by local authorities that have gone comprehensive, the school offers an escape route from the comprehensive system. Although the formula for a partially independent status worked out for voluntary-aided schools potentially offers a device for extending diversity and alternatives along other dimensions besides the religious one, and although alternatives can be envisaged which would be compatible with the aim of educating children of all abilities together, no developments in such directions have yet occurred.

In this respect the voluntary-aided schools offer an interesting contrast with Barnados, the National Children's Home and the Church of England Children's Society. The latter have inherited substantial capital assets and commitments from the same era and now depend for a lot of their funds on local authorities. But their current direction of development is towards pioneering and diversification – that is to extend what is done by the state rather than operate on the parallel bars principle.

## The Environment

The various local organisations active in the environmental field were noted in the last chapter. The National Trust, the county conservation trusts, the RSPB and the World Wildlife Fund together play a role in the conservation of the built and the natural environment that in terms of the sites, buildings and resources deployed probably exceeds that of the state. Beyond this all the environmental organisations seek to play a major part in educating the public, and with the exception of the National Trust, explicitly regard influencing statutory decisions as *an*, if not *the* essential function. Some, like the Ramblers, also give a prominent place to recreational activities that help their members to enjoy the environment.

In comparison with all the other fields examined here, this one is notable for the prominence of voluntary organisations that explicitly recognise themselves as pressure groups. No doubt this reflects in large measure the crucial part played in all environmental issues by government decision, particularly the way government uses its regulatory, planning powers. It is interesting nevertheless that in other fields where the state plays a no less prominent part, but by providing services rather than through regulating non-statutory activities, local voluntary organisations are much less inclined to don the mantle of pressure groups.

## Neighbourhood and Other Organisations

This chapter has not attempted to review the role of every voluntary organisation, even within the fields covered. However, there remain a number of groups of organisations that should not be ignored completely. Among them are those that seek to represent and act for the people of particular neighbourhoods. These were more numerous, absolutely as well as relatively, in Forgeham. The tenants' associations were mainly concerned to represent their members' interests to their common landlord, the council. However, there as elsewhere they also embarked on social and recreational activites. In addition, about half of the population of the town lived in areas covered by community associations. These enjoyed the use of community centres provided by the local authority for social, educational and recreational purposes, and received considerable organisational support from the adult and further education staff of the local authority. The main interests of these associations lay in the activities taking place in the centres. Nevertheless they do perhaps constitute the nearest urban counterpart to the statutory parish councils of rural areas.

Also noteworthy is a quite different category of organisation – those concerned to mobilise voluntary service without reference to any particular field of activity. Foremost among them is the WRVS; but Toc H and the various associations for professional people like Rotary and the Soroptimists should not be ignored. They do not find an obvious place in a field by field review of voluntary activities. Nevertheless they play a significant part in supporting the work of both voluntary organisations and statutory authorities by engaging the help of voluntary workers and by fund-raising efforts which often serve to set new projects in motion.

## The Views of the Consumer

There are three different standpoints or perspectives from which any publicly provided service can be appraised – that of the consumers or intended beneficiaries of the service, that of the providers or givers of the service, particularly the professional staff, and that of the policy-makers or providers of resources. According to the standpoint of the commentator, the weights accorded to different criteria are likely to vary; and certainly in practice judgements tend to be derived from different kinds of evidence.

In the case of voluntary organisations these standpoints are not so distinct and separable as in the case of statutory services. Thus with mutual aid organisations the three standpoints are conflated, except in so far as the organisation obtains resources from outside its membership, say through grant aid. However, the evidence deployed in this book is derived largely from people occupying only two out of the three standpoints — the service-givers and the policy-makers. This is usually true of discussions about the social services. Deference is paid to the importance of the consumers' views, but the difficulty of discovering what the consumers actually think tends to prevent an adequate recognition of their views. The Wolfenden Committee wished to take into account the views of the consumer, and was helped in this by the evidence it received from a number of mutual aid organisations. But the methodological problems involved and the large resources needed to overcome them precluded a substantial study in this field. Instead an effort was made to elicit opinions from consumers of services in the three towns. In each place this took the form of tape-recorded interviews, mostly carried out in clubs and day centres, with thirty or so individuals or groups drawn from the users of services for the elderly, the physically handicapped and mothers and children. The results are not quantifiable, but are of interest qualitatively, as illustrations of different points of view.

A major problem in obtaining views on services provided by voluntary organisations is that the term voluntary organisation is not one which has a well understood or widely shared meaning among the consumers of social services. Moreover the status of the organisation which provides the service is not always clear to its users, for example:

**Interviewer**
And do you know what organisation it is that runs this centre here?

**Respondent**
Well, I used to think it was something to do with the church but I believe now it is something to do with the council helping the aged (user of a day centre run by Age Concern with financial support from the local authority, Forgeham).

Another interview, also from Forgeham illustrates how
volunteers are often appreciated, but how their personal
characteristics may be more salient than the organisation
through which they come:

> **Interviewer** And does anyone ever visit you at home?
> **Respondent** No, not really. There is just a young girl
> who visits me. She started visiting me when she was at
> school, and she said that she took to me straight away.
> She is twenty-one now. She comes and does a bit of
> shopping for me. I've got a home help as well. You get a
> home help when you're old. She says she comes from
> the housing. I don't know really where they all come
> from; all I know is it's all to do with the old persons. My
> home help is very good. Of course, though, you just get
> used to one and then they change her . . . They used to
> send me children from the school to help me, but since
> I've moved, nobody's been. That's how the girl who
> comes to see me now came to see me first. She's very
> friendly. I like her coming but it was better when she
> was at school because she had more time.

One approach to appraising voluntary organisations from
a consumer perspective would be to obtain the views of
consumers using services comparable to each other except
for their voluntary or statutory status. This would yield the
firmest assessment of the voluntary factor *per se*. But most
voluntary organisations provide services that are different in
various ways and thus not strictly comparable. Consumers'
views on these are of no less interest, even if there is no
yardstick against which to make comparisons. A common
theme is simply gratitude and appreciation. Thus a
pensioner from Kirkforth on the hospital service:

> Lovely. They were very, very good. They were wonderful,
> very good, excellent. I can't say I enjoy hospital because
> I don't. But I enjoy the service. They did everything
> pleasantly.

And a mother from Anglebridge on her playgroup:

> Oh, it's wonderful. I'm very, very pleased with it. I just
> wish it was more often. It's very good because they have
> lots of friends up here which they probably wouldn't have
> at home, and it gives us a break and I think they enjoy it.

But this was far from the only sentiment. On a more critical
note are the following two views on voluntary organisations:

> Some of the people who come in are very nice and you can
> talk to them and they give a hand, but the ones who come
> in the evening, they more or less look on you as the 'poor
> unfortunates'. You know, they are all typically middle
> class, rolling in money, who think they are doing their bit
> for society. I think that's the way they look on it (resident
> of a women's refuge, Anglebridge).

> Well, I don't think all these things should be a charity.
> Instead of all these jumble sales and us having to beg to do
> things, I think they should all come out of the government.
> They spend enough money on other things . . . Places like
> this, it's all voluntary, and I think if there is any cutting
> down, it's these people whose money gets cut. Mind you,
> we are not asking for more than the normal family with
> the normal child at school. I mean you don't want charity
> and that's for sure (member of local Society for Mentally
> Handicapped Children, Anglebridge).

The first of these is a criticism of *de haut en bas* charity
and the second of the marginal status of voluntary provision.
Consumers are no less critical of statutory services, though
for different reasons. The fact that they are the main
providers and are publicly accountable for the way resources
are allocated means that statutory services are frequently in
the position of having to ration scarce resources. The
following quotation illustrates, perhaps in rather an extreme
form, the kind of story that can be told by those accorded a
low priority in the allocation of such resources:

> At the moment I am having a lot of trouble with the

council. I have been trying to get out of this house for two years and there's been all that trouble with the neighbour. I had a meeting with a councillor and he said that the best thing to do was to send a welfare woman down to see me. So they sent a welfare woman down to see me and she said she'd try as best as she could to get me out of this house. Anyway, that's as far as it went. The next thing that happened was that a house came empty down by my mother's. I wrote after it and they sent me a letter back saying I was not to write and not to phone any more. They said that when my time came up they'd see what they could do for me. That letter I get back every time. They just send you a standard letter; you don't get any further. I get really angry about it actually. I hear other women say that if I see a house empty I ought just to write after it; that's what they've done and they've just walked into a house. No questions asked. For myself I seem to have no luck with the council at all. I mean, six years I had to wait for this house and that was after I had the two babies. We had no hot water, we had to boil kettles, or boil a big pot on the stove for a good wash down. We had an outside toilet. We were overrun by mice. I had the health down two or three times and they couldn't get rid of them. I kept writing after a house and writing, but I never got any reply. They weren't bothered. As long as I had a roof over my head that was *all* that they cared about. Then, when I did go down to the council to accept the house, after they sent me the keys, even the welfare woman down there said, 'My God, Mrs B., have you been waiting as long as this to get a house?' They had a *pile* of my letters down there (Forgeham).

In contrast to impersonal rationing, voluntary organisations offer the opportunity to join in and share:

I think it's nice for all disabled people to share points of view, see how other poeple get on and if anything new comes out people can share them with each other. For example with cooking, some things you might be able to do, that you can't do now, if you knew about the gadgets and so on (member of a club for elderly handicapped,

Kirkforth).

When Claire was first born I knew there was a national society but I didn't know what I stood to gain from it. When Claire started school, I met one of the other mums. She told me all about it. There's a bungalow down at the coast and you can go down there for a holiday and for a very small cost. They do outings to the zoo, very little cost, sometimes it's nothing at all. There's all sorts of things. So since then I've become a committee member and I now encourage other parents to be a member of it (member of local Society for Mentally Handicapped Children, Anglebridge).

Finally, an eloquent testimony from a single mother in a voluntary hostel in Forgeham that is indicative of the effects of rationing on the rationers:

**Interviewer** As someone who has had to turn to various people for help in your situation, have you any particular views about whether things are better on the receiving end, if they are run by organisations in the system or more like this, by organisations which are outside the system and so not necessarily so controlled by local and central government?
**Respondent** Oh, they're far better outside the system. Definitely. It's far better if you're dealing with organisations that don't belong in any way either to local government or to central government.
**Interviewer** What makes you say that?
**Respondent** Because you do tend to be treated as an individual, a person. I don't know if these people — I mean social services and the housing department and so on — have so many dealings with people that they've become cynical or what. Perhaps they've got used to sob stories and to thinking it's not genuine. Anyway, whatever it is, they certainly don't want to know at all. As I said before, they don't think you've got any feelings and after all we *do* have feelings. Just because this sort of thing has happened to us, it doesn't mean that we have become lower forms of life. That's the thing that I've found most

traumatic, I think. I think I've felt that mainly from social services, social security and the housing department, from anybody I've seen there. It's not that I expect anybody to cry when I tell them that I haven't got anywhere to live, but at the same time I don't expect them just to say, 'Well, hard luck, hop it, you're wasting my time.'

**Interviewer** And who have you *not* felt that attitude from?

**Respondent** Housing Association, my own doctor, this organisation. That's all that I've really come into contact with. You see, I think that where people have a lot of rules to work by, for example, social security have to deal with a lot of red tape, and the Housing Corporation, they can't judge cases individually; they've just got a set of rules and that's it. They can't bend the rules. I suppose it's the same with all these things. In comparison with that, places like the Housing Association seem to take a real genuine concern in you. They really seem to want to help. I'm sure the other things when they started off were intended to do the same thing, but somehow it's all just become a system now. That's what I felt about the hospitals as well. It was competely impersonal. Perhaps if you pay it isn't so!

These illustrations are not presented as necessarily typical or representative of much larger numbers. However, they should not be dismissed out of hand, since they do exemplify understandable reactions to significant features of voluntary and statutory services. In particular they indicate two things. First, some, though not all, voluntary organisations offer an involvement which the statutory services cannot. Second, the rationing of resources, which is an inescapable statutory function, has wider consequences. The process of applying can be humiliating for the applicant, especially if in order to qualify for the resource it is necessary to reveal stigmatising personal circumstances. Beyond this, pressures are placed on people carrying out the rationing which make it difficult for them to see applicants as whole people with whom it is possible to empathise, rather than as an extra unit of demand. Indeed the impersonal and unbiased application of rules is an essential feature of bureaucracy. Not all statutory services operate in as bureaucratic a way as housing departments and supplementary benefit offices; professional social workers in particular offer a more personal and humane service. Nevertheless a rationing process of some sort cannot be avoided where demand substantially exceeds supply.

## Some Conclusions

This chapter has attempted to present a review field by field of the role of voluntary organisations. In attempting to summarise and appraise the situation it has not covered the activities of every voluntary organisation; rather it has aimed at delineating the main features. One conclusion which affects any attempt to generalise is that the role of the voluntary sector varies considerably from one field to another. Nevertheless one can usefully begin by asking how far the Webbs' extension ladder now accurately characterises the role of voluntary organisations. More specifically, to what extent has the state come to provide the foundations or framework of services, and the voluntary sector something extra, or to use the Webbs' words, the 'finer shades'?

In most of the fields discussed the state is clearly the main provider and does accept responsibility for basic levels and standards of provision. This is most conspicuously true of income support or the relief of destitution, the subject with which the Webbs were particularly concerned. But in important ways the term extension does indicate the nature of much of the contribution made by voluntary organisations. The advantages and disadvantages characteristic of voluntary provision noted by the Webbs also retain a lot of validity. The first of the advantages was 'invention and initiative'; though some voluntary organisations are small groups stuck in a rut, the pioneering role of voluntary organisations and their ability to respond flexibly to needs not readily catered for by established statutory structures have been noted at various points. Thus although invention and initiative are not the hallmarks of all voluntary organisations, the voluntary sector is a ready source of activities with these features. 'Their ability to lavish unstinted care on particular cases' was the second quality noted by the Webbs, and is borne out by the personal and caring character of much voluntary work, which is not constrained by the responsibilities carried by many statutory agencies for applying regulations and allocating resources between many competing claimants. Third, the Webbs mentioned 'the intensity and variety of the religious influences that they can bring to bear on personal character' — a phrase reflecting the strength of organised religion at that time and a preoccupation with moral improvement now largely absent. A religious inspiration is still present in many voluntary organisations, and more generally voluntary organisations remain a vehicle for the expression of public service and of strong personal commitments and charismatic influences that do not find an easy place in large bureaucracies.

On the negative side of any assessment of the voluntary sector the Webbs pointed with powerful logic to the characteristics of voluntary organisations which prevent them being vehicles for the provision of expensive universal services available to all those eligible. These require bureaucratic organisations acting with statutory authority, and can only be funded from taxation. The Webbs also noted that voluntary organisations were unevenly distributed and that their incidence reflected particular enthusiasms and commitments rather than a distribution corresponding to the needs that might be discovered by an impartial survey. Beyond this, attracting resources occupied a lot of their energies and still does today, as witness the fact that lack of money or volunteers were the problems most frequently reported by voluntary organisations responding to the Wolfenden Committee questionnaire.

The Webbs' analysis does not apply across the board, and two fields in particular constitute clear exceptions. Advice, information and counselling are mainly provided by voluntary organisations, as is care for those with special housing needs. The state accepts some responsibilities in these fields. It provides some information, advice and counselling itself, particularly through SSDs, and funds some of the voluntary providers of it, in particular the Citizens' Advice Bureaux. Likewise the recent Homeless Persons Act has clarified statutory responsibilities for the homeless. But voluntary organisations, again with financial support from the state, are the main providers for those with special needs.

Does this mean, it may be asked, that the relationship between the state and the voluntary sector in some fields remains that of the parallel bars rejected by the Webbs? In a few instances the voluntary sector can still be seen as offering a better service to a more deserving population; this is a not unrealistic description of the role of some voluntary-aided schools and of some voluntary homes for the elderly. But this does not apply to the two main exceptions noted above. In the case of counselling and advice the voluntary sector offers a service widely used by all sectors of the population. In the case of housing, local authorities cater for the large proportion of families and the elderly whose needs are not met by the private sector; while the voluntary sector serves those with special needs, in many respects the most deprived part of the population.

One interpretation of these departures from the extension ladder model might be to view them as anomalies, which will be rectified in the course of further development. However, there are good reasons why provision in both fields should retain a measure of independence. As argued earlier, voluntary services for the homeless can mobilise commitments and maintain a flexibility of operation in a manner difficult to achieve in a statutory setting, while the consumers of statutory services will be in an unsatisfactory position if their only source of advice about those services is the self-same services.

Hence the extension ladder, while it conveys a lot about current voluntary and statutory roles, does not adequately pinpoint all the salient features of the situation. In particular, as is hardly surprising, it does not take into account the implications of the great extensions of the statutory services which have taken place since the model was propounded and brought the level of public expenditure on social and environmental services in 1977 to 34 per cent of the national income. [14] The voluntary organisations discussed by the Webbs were those defined in Chapter 2 as volunteer organisations and funded charities. Mutual aid organisations and the special agencies have appeared on the scene since that time. They both reflect limitations to statutory action made evident by its growth.

The extent and complexity, and indeed the power, of

statutory agencies means that those affected by them need to exert a countervailing influence if the services are to respond sensitively to their needs. But more than just protection and the representation of their interests, they and the public in general also seek a more positive involvement, as givers of care and decision-makers, not simply as passive recipients. Hence all the discussion of involvement and participation, the growth of mutual aid and community care, the statutory encouragement of community development and the funding by the state of activities which it cannot readily carry out itself. In this context voluntary organisations constitute *the* essential medium for organised mutual aid, and *an* essential channel for the involvement of the community in caring activities.

In the light of these developments new issues need to be brought to the fore about the relative roles of statutory and voluntary sectors. The argument over extension ladders and parallel bars was about whether the state should play a central role. The essential questions now are about the nature of the relationship between statutory, voluntary and informal sectors. These are posed by asking whether voluntary action is merely marginal to the statutory services, or whether it plays an integral part in service provision. Thus one can speak of alternative models, the marginal and the integral, which serve to encapsulate the issues presently most relevant to the future role of the voluntary sector. To these we return in the next chapter.

### Notes

1. S. and B. Webb, *The Prevention of Destitution* (Longmans, 1912).
2. Lord Beveridge, *Voluntary Action* (Allen and Unwin, 1948).
3. Department of Health and Social Security, *Health and Personal Social Services Statistics for England* (HMSO, 1977), Tables 7.1, 7.4, 7.5 and 7.13.
4. For a discussion of relative costs see S. Hatch and I. Mocroft, 'The Relative Costs of Services Provided by Voluntary and Statutory Organisations', *Public Administration* (forthcoming).
5. British Association of Social Workers, *The Social Work Task* (BASW Publications, 1977), para 3.11.
6. E. M. Goldberg, *Social Work since Seebohm: All Things to All Men?* (National Institute for Social Work, 1979), p. 9.
7. J. Heisler and A. Whitehouse, 'The NMGC Client', *Marriage Guidance* (November/December, 1976).

8.   B. Abel-Smith, M. Zander and R. Brooke, *Legal Problems and the Citizen* (Heinemann, 1973), Ch. 5.

9.   Personal Communication from Dr Richard Fox, Severalls Hospital, Colchester.

10.   Office of Population Census and Surveys, *Mortality Statistics 1976* (HMSO, 1978), Table 9.

11.   Goldberg, *Social Work since Seebohm, p. 5.*

12.   *Adult Education: a Plan for Development* (HMSO, 1973).

13.   See notably M. Bone and E. Ross, *The Youth Service and Similar Provision for Young People* (HMSO, 1972); J. Eggleston, *Adolescence and Community: the Youth Service in Britain* (Edward Arnold, 1976);  M. Thomas and J. Perry, *National Voluntary Youth Organisations* (PEP, 1975).

14.   Central Statistical Office, *National Income and Expenditure, 1967-1977* (HMSO).

# 6 DEVELOPMENT AND ACCOUNTABILITY: THE VOLUNTARY SECTOR AND LOCAL GOVERNMENT

The conclusion of the last chapter was that the main issues concerning the role of the voluntary sector now mostly come down to questions about the interrelationships between it and government. This chapter seeks to explore these interrelationships at local level. They are usually the products of gradual evolution, rather than clearly defined policy, and the language in which they are discussed is something of a jumble of concepts that mean different things to different people. In particular there are two terms — accountability and co-ordination — much used in this context that need to be clarified if any analysis of the situation is to be fruitful. Both are ways of talking about the relationship between individual organisations and their environment of beneficiaries and other services. The chapter begins by examining these concepts in turn. It argues that different forms of accountability apply to different types of organisations, and that co-ordination should be interpreted more positively as development. Next it describes the pattern of relationships in the three towns, concluding with an appraisal of them in the light of the models put forward in the last chapter.

## Accountability

Accountability can refer to several things. In the narrowest sense it means avoiding malpractice and keeping the accounts properly. This raises problems more of practice than of principle, though these can be difficult in the case of some less well established organisations. More substantially, accountability refers to the effective use of resources for the purposes for which they were provided. In this sense it means much the same as responsibility. In the third sense it refers to the relationships between an organisation and those it seeks to represent or on whose behalf it claims to act. Here a more exact meaning is conveyed by the term legitimacy. It is the last two senses that will be discussed mainly in this chapter.

Local government has a well understood basis upon which its legitimacy rests, and established mechanisms for ensuring responsible action. Authority lies with the councillors and is exercised particularly through the control of expenditure. Councillors owe their position to an election in which all adults can participate. Under them are hierarchies which translate decisions into action downwards and maintain a surveillance to ensure that tasks are properly carried out. Sanctions can be exerted against those in the hierarchies to ensure that instructions are carried out. There are a number of criticisms that can be made of this process. In casting their votes in local elections the electors are more influenced by national considerations than by local ones. Thus local elections are only to a limited extent judgements on the performance of the local authority, and effectively the choice of councillors lies with the small number of party activists who select the candidates. And even in so far as the councillors are the people's choice, the officials may have a major influence on what policies are adopted and effective control over how they are implemented. The councillors may have limited time, knowledge and capabilities; they may not be in close contact with those they represent, and so on. Nevertheless the machinery of representative democracy is there, is reasonably well understood and works after a fashion.

Voluntary organisations are in a quite different position. Their legitimacy is not sanctioned by widespread popular participation. Moreover within the limited constituencies which they serve there is not much involvement. Trade unions, which are in some ways analogous, at least have the mechanisms for ensuring legitimacy and responsibility, even if they are not always well used. However, these differences do not render any discussion of the accountability of voluntary organisations nugatory. All voluntary organisations can be seen as mobilising resources in pursuit of objectives,

and the discussion can best be pursued by asking about the
constraints that affect their use of resources. As pointed out
in Chapter 2, the nature and the source of their resources
varies and provides a basis for classifying organisations. A
distinction was made between organisations dependent
primarily on voluntary effort and those dependent on finance
for the employment of staff. The former were divided into
mutual aid associations and volunteer organisations, and the
latter into special agencies dependent on grants and funded
charities dependent on charitable donations and charges for
services.

In the case of organisations dependent on people working
voluntarily, which comprise the great majority of local
voluntary organisations, it is their own time that the
participants are using. It may be that they are inefficient or
misguided; and indeed the reliability of voluntarily run
organisations is a problem commonly encountered by those
who have to relate to them. But how they use their time is
not something which can be subjected to formal sanctions;
nor does it readily lend itself to sophisticated forms of
accountability. For example, careful record-keeping may be
regarded by volunteers as red tape and an infringement of the
essential spontaneity of voluntary action. In this situation it
is the motives of volunteers that have to be understood and
if necessary influenced. Given the right approach it may be
possible to improve standards and monitor performance. But
this has to take place by a process of development, which is
considered later in the chapter. Beyond this, if an
organisation is interpreting its objectives inappropriately or
pursuing them ineffectively, another organisation can be set
up instead. As was shown in Chapter 4, there is a high rate of
births and deaths among voluntary organisations. This is a
source of change, as much as development within
organisations. It places voluntary organisations in a market
rather than in a planned situation, where competition is as
influential as administrative decisions. Of course some kinds
of organisations are more easily set up than others. While a
new playgroup or pensioners' club can readily be brought
into being, the idea of, say, two societies for mentally
handicapped children in one town makes less sense; the local
support for such duplication would be limited and the

national organisation probably would not recognise the competitor. However, an action group may serve to introduce a new impetus and to bring about needed change. The Disabled Action Group in Forgeham is an illustration of this kind of device.

Duplication is a criticism not infrequently levelled at the voluntary sector, particularly by people familiar with statutory services where overlapping responsibilities tend to be seen as very undesirable, and where whatever the inertia, there are clearly understood mechanisms for re-allocating responsibilities. In the voluntary sector, however, duplication can serve a useful function as a source of change as well as of choice and variety. Of course this is not always so, and it can be wasteful of resources. The point is that duplication in the two sectors should be seen in a different light. Thus the voluntary sector cannot be subjected to the same sort of planning as the statutory sector.

Accountability tends to become more of an issue with special agencies. Against such organisations the grant-giving authority can readily apply sanctions by withdrawing its grant. This can place it in a stronger position *vis-à-vis* the staff of special agencies than it is *vis-à-vis* its own employees. In the three towns special agencies were few in number, and usually it did not seem to be difficult for representatives of the authority giving the grant to make judgements about and influence the work of the organisation, either by sitting on the organisation's committee or through liaising with it on day-to-day issues. However, the larger organisations in Forgeham, which are not untypical of the new kind of voluntary organisation growing up in inner-city areas, were beginning to constitute an exception. The main ones were the Community Relations Council, the Crypt and the now defunct YVFF project. These were difficult for an outside grant-giver to know about fully. Partly this was because they obtained grants and sponsorship from various sources. Partly also their independence and consequently the scope for more unorthodox forms of service was one of the justifications for their existence, and an argument against too close scrutiny. Such situations certainly contain the seeds of conflict, and of a conflict in which questions about the effectiveness and accountability of the voluntary organisation cannot readily be

disentangled from questions about the desirability of its
objectives. Skill on the part of voluntary organisation staff
and the local authority officials who relate to the organisation
may limit the conflict; but it would be a mistake to think that
improved formulae for ensuring accountability can avoid
conflict situations in the case of organisations that obtain
grants to work in controversial fields.

The blind institute in Forgeham was a funded charity and
in a somewhat different category. Most of its resources came
from its own fund-raising or inherited assets, and its problems
lay in being behind rather than ahead of developments in the
statutory services. Here the case was not one of possible
misuse of the ratepayers' money, nor was it one of
misappropriation of charitable funds, but of whether the
resources were being used in the best way possible from the
point of view of the interests of the blind people in the town.
As with other organisations of this kind, resources tend to be
given because of the appeal of the cause; this relieves such
organisations from close public scrutiny, leaving only the
Charity Commission as a long stop in case things go badly
wrong. This means that the quality of its performance
depends on the organisation's own internal dynamic, rather
than outside pressures, whether from other agencies or the
intended beneficiaries. Some organisations of this kind, like
the Spastics Society establishment described in Chapter 3,
have a strong and progressive internal dynamic that puts their
independence to good use, but not all.

To summarise the discussion so far, many of the
organisations depending on volunteers are in a fairly open and
fluid situation; change can be brought about through the
formation of new organisations or development work directed
particularly to the motivation of the volunteers. Organisations
dependent on grants can in addition be subjected to negative
sanctions. Funded charities are most likely to be immune to
outside influences.

As regards legitimacy, when voluntary organisations are
simply providing a service, the question 'by what right do you
provide the service?' can be answered in two ways: either the
recipients want it, or if they do not want it, the voluntary
organisation is acting as the agent of the state. In between
there is a grey area where people may be cajoled into wanting

a service, for example the isolated elderly person who 'needs' visiting. In this situation the voluntary organisation is acting no less legitimately than the evangelist, and arguably more legitimately than the salesman who is seeking his own pecuniary gain.

The legitimacy of voluntary organisations tends to become more controversial when they claim to act or speak for others and to represent them as a pressure group. Here they come into conflict with the councillors who are elected as representatives of an area. The right of people to express their views cannot be denied in a society with any respect for civil liberties. However, the weight that ought to be attached to such views must be affected by how far they do in fact reflect what the people being spoken for think. Here mutual aid associations are on strong ground. The position of other kinds of voluntary organisation might be strengthened if ways were found of including their intended beneficiaries in their decision-making processes. Otherwise it rests simply on the weight of their evidence and the strength of their reasoning.

In the three towns we found no evidence of any searching discussion of accountability, either in the sense of legitimacy or of responsibility. It is not possible to say how far this lack of interest in alternative sources of legitimacy and better ways of maintaining effectiveness was due to lack of imagination, to objection by the staff of voluntary organisations to any constraint on their autonomy or to anxiety on the part of statutory authorities that alternative sources of legitimacy might threaten their own.

## Co-ordination and Development

The case for co-ordination within the voluntary sector was put long ago by the Webbs, who in commending the pre-1914 growth of Guilds of Help argued:

> The Guild . . . would have for its function, not any separate philosophy of its own, but the co-ordination and promotion of the work of each of its parts . . . the Council of the Guild of Help would, in fact, be the channel through which all the suggestiveness and inventiveness and devotion

of the outside public would be brought to bear on the
municipality in such a way as to raise the standard of
thought and feeling among the elected representatives and
officials to whom the community committed its work. [1]

These arguments were elaborated and restated in the
Wolfenden Report, [2] which in order to promote fresh
thinking coined the term 'intermediary functions' to denote
a variety of ways of supporting voluntary action and linking
it with the statutory services. The main functions the report
identified under this heading were development, support
services, liaison and representation; and among them it gave
priority to development. The various organisations carrying
out some or all of these functions were divided into the local
and the national and the specialist (covering one field only)
and the generalist.

There is little purpose in recapitulating here the extensive
discussion in the report. However, a few points can be stated
briefly. Although the large voluntary organisations with a
strong national structure may have little need for outside
help at the local level, most local voluntary organisations are
small and rather frail. As suggested by the analysis of the
formation of new organisations in Chapter 4, outside support
plays a considerable part in their development. Often very
specific in their interests, they tend to lack the knowledge
and skills to see the problem with which they are concerned
in a wider perspective, to relate effectively to other agencies
and to maximise their impact.

All these are arguments for putting resources into the
development of the voluntary sector. On the voluntary side,
the main organisations in a position to carry this out are the
councils of voluntary service (CVS), the successors of the
Guilds supported by the Webbs. Often associated with them
are volunteer bureaux, which constitute a recently established
national network. CVS used to describe themselves as
co-ordinating bodies, which implies a constraining rather than
a developmental and promotional role in relation to other
organisations; but this term now seems to be dying in line
with a more positive interpretation of their role, which could
make them the instrument of collective action by voluntary
organisations to create conditions conducive to their own

development.

On the statutory side, SSDs and hospitals during the past decade have created numerous posts for individuals with the job of liaising with voluntary organisations and promoting the recruitment and use of volunteers. In addition there is a growing number of people described as community workers, nearly all employed either directly by local authorities or by organisations dependent on grants from statutory authorities. Some of their work lies in the field of community organisation, i.e. of relations between agencies, under consideration here. More of it, however, is concerned with community development, or helping individuals to organise in pursuit of common goals.

## Intermediary Functions in the Three Towns

Intermediary functions are being carried out in each of the towns, but not on a very systematic basis. In *Kirkforth* a senior member of the social services department divisional staff gave about a quarter of his time to developing the use of volunteers and relating to voluntary organisations, supported by an assistant mainly concerned with the use of volunteers within the department. Based in the main local hospital was a volunteer organiser, also with an assistant. Besides recruiting a substantial number of volunteers to work in the hospitals, they had played a major part in setting up a stroke club and a talking newspaper for the blind. On the voluntary side was the recently formed council of voluntary service, mentioned in Chapter 3. Its workers were pursuing a variety of initiatives. But their inexperience and the change-over of staff meant that the CVS was not able to develop that reservoir of information and personal contacts that are necessary for the successful performance of intermediary functions; and by the time of writing the organisation had gone out of existence.

The personnel discussed so far all operated across a broad field. In addition, though there was not a strong pattern of organisations coming together on the basis of specific interest, there were some arrangements to promote this. The social services department called meetings from time to time of organisations concerned with a particular client group for purposes of consultation. Besides this, a forum concerned with old people met quarterly to discuss such matters as bus passes for the elderly and arrangements for obtaining medical prescriptions. The forum did not, however, include the pensioners' clubs. There seemed to be more positive activity in relation to playgroups, where the SSD playgroup organiser and the local Pre-school Playgroups Association were together encouraging the formation of new playgroups.

The SSD liaison officer complained, 'when I suggest to people that they can make things happen, they say, "You don't understand Kirkforth. Things don't happen that fast here." ' Perhaps he was right in suggesting that the town was too conservative and lacking in dynamism to generate a vigorous collective effort on the part of the voluntary sector. However, his own judgement on the ineffectiveness of the CVS had certainly influenced the SSD in deciding to give little financial support to it. Consequently, the capability for performing intermediary functions was largely left in the hands of himself and the hospital volunteer organisers.

In *Anglebridge* the situation was not dissimilar. The SSD area team had an officer whose main job was relating to voluntary organisations and encouraging neighbourhood care schemes. Although there was no volunteer organiser in the hospitals, there was more activity on the part of voluntary organisations. As noted earlier, there was an impressive range of organisations in Anglebridge concerned with the physically handicapped. Most of these were linked through the Association for the Physically Handicapped, which over the years had been responsible for a number of initiatives designed to respond to unmet needs. The local Age Concern, supported by the county organisation which was also located in Anglebridge, was active in its field. The fact that Anglebridge is the county town was also reflected in the presence there of the county community council. Its main responsibilities lay outside the social services, but as a subsidiary activity it did provide a limited volunteer bureau service. Another initiative emanating from the voluntary sector should also be mentioned. At the time of our first survey, under the impetus of the local diocesan social welfare agency, a standing conference of voluntary organisations had been formed. This produced a directory of local organisations, but lacking a clear sense of purpose and any staff of its own, it had faded out by the time of our second survey. There then remained, as a regular meeting point for voluntary organisations, only monthly lunches organised by the head of the SSD area team.

Thus in Anglebridge and Kirkforth initiatives had been taken to establish a voluntary intermediary body, but had not been sufficiently vigorous or widely supported to make them a success. In *Forgeham* the idea of establishing a local CVS had been discussed on various occasions, but the discussions had never led to any further action. There was a fear that such an organisation might come between the local authority and individual organisations, and on one occasion the emissary who had come to expound the idea created an unfavourable impression. One of the people we interviewed attributed this firmly to the parochialism of Forgeham itself and of its voluntary organisations. By the time of our second survey, however, a new situation had been created by the government's Inner Cities Programme. This called for public involvement and faced council officers with the problem of there being no umbrella organisation and thus no obvious medium for securing the participation of voluntary organisations. Consequently a steering committee was established, composed mainly of individuals from the more active voluntary organisations. At the time of writing this seems to be leading to the formation of a CVS or of an organisation carrying out similar intermediary functions. Forgeham is one of very few towns of its size without an organisation of this kind. What it does have, however, is a number of more or less formal groups concerned with particular fields and a committee of the local authority established to carry on liaison with voluntary organisations. The membership of the committee is not for the most part drawn from among the more influential councillors, but it does invite to its meetings the representatives of organisations with common interests, and issues emerging in the discussions can be followed up.

The more specific groupings of voluntary organisations include the following — an action group concerned with homelessness, an informal grouping of organisations offering counselling services, a federation of tenants' associations, an active Age Concern, and under the auspices of the Education Department a federation of community associations. Largest among the umbrella bodies in Forgeham is the Community Relations Council, which has a number of projects of its own as well as linking and seeking to speak for the ethnic organisations in the town. Also notable in this context is a project established by the Young Volunteer Force Foundation (now the Community Projects Foundation) in 1969. Initially this was an attempt to mobilise young volunteers, but it evolved into a community action agency that launched initiatives in a number of deprived areas. By the time of our second survey the local authority had decided not to go on supporting the project as a whole, and there was left behind only a local advice centre. Thus it followed a course similar to that of the contemporaneous Home Office Community Development Projects.

On the statutory side the number of individuals with responsibilities for relating to the voluntary sector is limited. There is no volunteer organiser in the hospitals. In the SSD, besides a playgroup organiser, one of the assistant directors includes among his tasks maintaining relationships with voluntary organisations. Within the limits of the time he can give to this part of his work, he interprets his responsibilities positively and is a recognised link point among the voluntary organisations. There is also a small number of councillors who are active in this context.

The existence of the various groupings of voluntary organisations in Forgeham is an expression of the need for some medium for collective action among them, but a recognised framework and the staff who might support and service such groupings of voluntary organisations are lacking. In Anglebridge and Kirkforth the need for a voluntary intermediary body is less evident. Being smaller places the case for formal machinery to promote initiatives at that level rather than at county level seems less. The arguments for formal machinery must depend on more general views of the potentialities of the voluntary sector and of the best means of realising those potentialities.

## Grants

It is surprisingly difficult to gain an accurate and comparable picture of the grants made by local authorities to voluntary organisations. This is partly because outside the metropolitan counties there are two different local authorities, and within each local authority several different committees which give grants. Practices vary between authorities; for example, the same organisation may well come under different committees in different authorities, and what in one authority may be treated as an agency payment may in another be treated as a grant. In addition, as well as giving financial support, local authorities provide resources in kind. For example, an organisation which gets a grant covering rent of premises in one area may in another get a smaller grant but free premises. The largest resources provided in kind were in Forgeham, where the SSD and the Education Department each seconded some half a dozen full-time staff to work with and under the day-to-day direction of voluntary organisations. The salaries of the staff employed by the CAB and the costs of its offices were also met in this way. Recently, too, the Manpower Services Commission has entered the field as a source of statutory grants which bypasses the local authorities. These are some of the reasons why more explicit and exact statistical data are missing from this acount: a summary, however, can be attempted.

The following discussion takes no account of charges paid in respect of individuals receiving residential care from voluntary organisations, nor of grants made by education departments. The county social services committees for both Anglebridge and Kirkforth have a subcommittee which considers grants to voluntary organisations and which in each county in 1977/8 awarded grants that amounted to 8p *per capita* of the county population. Most of the money went to county-wide organisations like those for the physically handicapped, Age Concern and diocesan social welfare agencies, and in essence enabled such organisations to employ staff. In addition there were a large number of smaller grants, many of them to assist local agencies and clubs with their running costs, made in the light of advice from the SSD's area or divisional office. A further category of small grants really amounted to donations to good causes.

The Kirkforth District Council provides grants at a somewhat higher level, amounting to 17p *per capita* to organisations within the fields covered by this study. A major part of this sum is accounted for by grants to pensioners' clubs, including a subvention made according to an agreed formula by the county council (not counted in the 8p mentioned in the preceding paragraph). The rest of the sum is attributable largely to grants to voluntary organisations forming the local branches of a national service, notably the CAB and Marriage Guidance, plus a number of smaller sums. In Anglebridge the situation is similar, with the major exception that grants are not made to pensioners' clubs. In consequence grant aid there amounted to only some 6p *per capita.*

In Forgeham the level of grant aid was higher than in the other two towns, but still low in comparison to other metropolitan districts. In 1978/9 grants awarded by the SSD amounted to 29p *per capita.* Ten of them exceeded £3,000; four of these went to hostels catering for special needs and two to community projects, the others being the blind institute, Age Concern, MGC and playgroups generally. The only other major grant outside the fields of the SSD and the Education Department was to the Community Relations Council, which amounted to some 4p *per capita.* Allowances should also be made for the secondments mentioned above.

The leading members and officers of all the local authorities covering the three towns could be relied upon to make public statements about the value of voluntary effort. But if one makes a critical review of what they do it is difficult to maintain that public sentiments are matched by action. Indeed public sentiments are sometimes belied by private criticisms of the weakness or nuisance value of voluntary organisations. Judging by the proceedings of the Social Services Committee of the county council for Anglebridge, members and officers did give serious and sympathetic attention to problems raised by voluntary organisations. The county's main and quite substantial investment in the voluntary sector takes the form of the liaison officers based in each of the 14 area teams, the benefit of whose work seemed to be judged mainly in terms of the number of

volunteers working for or with the department. In Kirkforth
the county council proceedings did not give the same
indication of positive interest, and the input of staff time
represented by its liaison officers was less. Indeed one of the
reasons given for refusing a grant to the county Pre-school
Playgroups Association, that the resources could be better
used through the county's own playgroup organisers, seemed
more indicative of the general approach.

In Forgeham, as one might expect of an authority in area
and population much smaller than the two counties,
relationships between the voluntary sector and the authority
were more intimate. Among the members and officers there
were individuals willing to involve themselves actively and
supportively with voluntary organisations and argue for them
with their colleagues. But the dominant attitude among
members and officers seemed to be one of pride in the
municipality, leading on to the assumption that, though
voluntary organisations might help in various ways, the more
effective and less troublesome answer to most problems lay
in municipal action rather than in the development of
partnerships with the voluntary sector.

**Marginal or Integral?**

The previous chapter raised the question of whether the
position of voluntary organisations was marginal or integral
in relation to statutory services. This can be examined in two
ways, either by looking at the relative size of the sectors and
the relationships between them in different fields or, as in
this chapter, by taking a more general view of the interface
between the voluntary sector and local government.
Considered field by field, voluntary organisations are more
than marginal in advice and counselling and in caring for the
single homeless, since they are the main providers. Much of
the funding for the voluntary organisations concerned comes
from statutory sources, but funds have been granted in a
rather *ad hoc* way in response to particular needs and there
has certainly not been a developed joint approach. Thus the
voluntary sector is something more than marginal but less
than integral. With provision for youth and the under-fives,

however, the voluntary sector does make a substantial
contribution and there are usually arrangements which
generate a joint, more integral approach.

In other fields, notably schooling and in most of the health
services, the voluntary sector is definitely in a marginal
situation. Its proportionately small, supplementary
contribution may be welcome, but it is nowhere near the
centre of things. Community health councils could in time
give voluntary organisations more say in the health service,
but in the three towns at any rate their influence had not
reached the point at which it might contradict what has just
been said. The role of voluntary organisations in caring for
the elderly and the handicapped is in quantitative terms
proportionately greater, and where there was a lively Age
Concern or association for the disabled it did seem to weigh
rather more heavily in statutory thinking. Thus with the
personal social services there are signs of movement away
from a marginal position.

Looking at the sectors as a whole, in some places more has
been done to develop the voluntary sector than in the three
towns. But they seem not untypical of the general picture.
In them the support for the voluntary sector from the
statutory sector as measured by grants and other material
resources was very modest. Support in terms of staff time
and interest was not insignificant, but was largely confined to
individuals occupying a few key roles, rather than being
automatically an element in the work of many staff. But
perhaps more significant than anything else was the very
limited recognition of the need for development within the
voluntary sector. In none of the towns was there a strong
generalist intermediary body. It was suggested earlier that
judgements as to the need for such a body were bound to
reflect wider views about the role of the voluntary sector. If
it is accorded only a marginal status, the various intermediary
functions do not have a high priority and can be left to
designated officials. If, on the other hand, an integral position
is aimed at, significant resources and an effective generalist
agency are needed to ensure that the voluntary sector can
think and act for itself, rather than being the creature of the
statutory services. It becomes important, too, not to ignore
problems of accountability and legitimacy, and to seek new

ways of making them a reality.

As stated at the beginning, this book makes no claim to be advancing a plan for the development of the voluntary sector. However, at various points the potentialities of the voluntary sector have been noted, and the drift of the argument clearly supports a more integral relationship between the sectors. In this it echoes a quite widespread and growing body of opinion. Nevertheless it would be wrong to conclude this chapter simply on a hortatory note, without noting some of the objections and obstacles that lie in the way of developments in this direction.

Some of the obstacles relate to attitudes and philosophy. At one level the aspirations of statutory services can be interpreted negatively as a desire for empire-building, for the enhanced status that comes from larger budgets, more staff and wider responsibilities. Such desires are met by extending statutory services, not by supporting voluntary organisations. At a more principled level many people make a stand on the issue of representative democracy. On this line of argument only local and central government are adequately accountable to the public, and quite apart from issues of effectiveness, reliance on voluntary organisations involves an abdication of responsibility to special interests. In the past this argument was applied particularly to the class bias in the membership and attitudes of voluntary organisations; currently it is directed also at manifestations of community action on behalf of deprived groups. This is not the place for an extended discussion of pluralism. Suffice it to say that criticisms of the kind indicated at the beginning of this chapter can readily be levelled at the workings of representative democracy. These indicate that it is not immune from manipulation by special interests, and point to more open forms of government and a recognition of voluntary organisations as legitimate critics and participants in decision-making and service provision as ways of enhancing rather than eroding democracy. Thus the integral model of the role of the voluntary sector does rest upon a philosophy of participatory pluralism, incompatible with a narrow and exclusive adherence to the traditional forms of representative democracy.

At the more practical level of the working of institutions

there remain unresolved questions as to the feasibility of a more integral model. These relate to the arrangements by which wider participation in decision-making and service delivery can be secured. There is now a decade of experience of attempts at public participation in decision-making, mostly related to environmental planning, during which participation has become more widely accepted and the different ways of facilitating it better understood.

Participation in service provision is less contentious. Yet for all the advocacy of community care and the promotion of volunteering, it seems as yet to have been pursued with less effect. The proliferation of neighbourhood care schemes and of mutual aid organisations are evidence of a widespread willingness to participate. However, well substantiated evidence about the benefits of such activities has been slow to emerge. There are a variety of concrete questions to which answers are needed. To take one example, to what extent and in what circumstances can neighbourhood care schemes reduce or postpone the need for residential care for elderly people? With the prospect of increasing numbers of infirm elderly, research is now being devoted to such issues, and before long is likely to begin to come up with some of the answers. Looking at it the other way round, a marginal contribution from the voluntary sector can be accommodated by the statutory sector without a major change in its *modus operandi*, although a larger contribution could well have major implications, particularly for the degree of decentralisation and the way professionals interpret their roles. There is here a major agenda for research and development, to say nothing of changes in public expectations.

## Notes

1. S. and B. Webb, *The Prevention of Destitution* (Longmans, 1912), pp. 259-60.
2. *The Future of Voluntary Organisations* (Croom Helm, 1977), especially Chapters 6, 7 and 10.

# 7    IN A WIDER PERSPECTIVE

Britain is notable among non-Communist countries for combining extensive and centrally controlled statutory services with a very high level of concentration in the private sector of the economy. Ours is a highly administered and oligopolistic society. Decision-making is in the hands of relatively few institutions and individuals, and there is little scope for small-scale enterprise. Once famous for their readiness to queue, the British people have until recently acquiesced surprisingly willingly in the benevolently intended regulation of their lives.

Now contrary pressures are making themselves felt. These take many forms. Politically, they find expression in demands for participation and devolution, in attacks on bureaucracy and in the advocacy of small business. And more directly people have been seeking to escape from the main statutory and commercial structures by establishing activities outside them. The term 'the informal economy' has recently come into use to denote many of them. Some are illegal; pilfering has been estimated as 2 or 3 per cent of all production, [1] and it has been suggested that earnings that evade the tax net amount to 7.5 per cent of the gross domestic product. [2] Neither estimate is well substantiated, but they indicate that these expressions of the informal economy are not insignificant. Other aspects of it, such as 'do-it-yourself' housework and reciprocal exchanges of goods and more particularly services, represent legitimate additions to the sum of economic activity but find no place in any computation of the gross national product since they do not involve cash transactions.

On the border of what is known to official statisticians are such ventures as industrial and housing co-operatives and various essays in pursuit of alternative patterns of living. These range from attempts to recapture the simple virtues of rural life, through more or less formalised experiments in communal living that represent escapes from the nuclear family, to experiments in the development of alternative sources of energy and alternative forms of health care. Diverse as they are, legal and illegal, included or excluded from official computations, purposive and ideological or spontaneous and adaptive, Utopian or practical and self-interested, they share with the subject-matter of this book the characteristic of being outside the state and outside the mainstream of capitalist enterprise.

Most of these activities raise questions as to the validity of the indicators commonly employed to measure social conditions and the progress of the economy. What, for example, is the significance of the figures for unemployment if many of those registered as unemployed are busily engaged on private fiddles? How valid are official data on production and productivity if many people add substantially to their economic welfare by providing services on a reciprocal basis?

Although these phenomena are not new, interest in them is recent and takes various forms. One set of reactions is negative. It concentrates on the illegal aspects of the informal economy and points to the possibility that the informal activity may cause jobs to be lost in the formal economy. Such attitudes found expression in the attack on the 'lump' in the building industry. Other responses view the informal economy in a more positive light. Thus it can be seen as a response to constraints and rigidities in the formal economy, and a source of work not available at all in the formal economy. More optimistically, its growth can be interpreted not just as a case of *faute de mieux*, but as at least a partial answer to the failings of the British economy, and as a signpost towards the economy of the future in which much routine, alienating employment will have been rendered unnecessary by microprocessors.

If one is seeking the counterpart of the informal economy in the social welfare field, it may be identified as comprising the transactions that find no place in the national accounts. This means it includes both the informal sector as defined in Chapter 2 and the voluntary work part of the voluntary sector. As such it differs in significant respects from the informal economy in general. First, none of it is illegal; it involves no financial transactions concealed from the authorities; indeed the essence of it is services for which the giver is not paid. Second, a substantial element of it takes an organised form through voluntary organisations. Third, whereas the informal economy generally provides goods and services that would have to be paid for if obtained through the formal economy, informal and voluntary sources of social welfare provision offer services that would be free if obtained from the state. Obviously this affects people's willingness to exchange one for the other.

For these reasons it would be a mistake to treat the informal economy as exactly comparable to informal/ voluntary sources of social welfare. Nevertheless they are not unrelated. The apparent growth of both betokens dissatisfaction with working for and getting services from large formal organisations. And looking to the future, it is possible to envisage a society in which shortening hours of employment will enable people to spend more time on voluntary, home and community-based activities of all kinds. Recent trends have been towards more and more women entering the formal economy, but overall the supply of labour now substantially exceeds the demand for it, and promises to exceed it even more in future. It is important to ask whether the consequences of this surplus can be spread about and enjoyed by many as leisure, instead of being inflicted on a minority as unemployment. One is at risk, in pursuing a discussion of this kind, of fabricating a new Utopia. That is not the aim of this book. But it is reasonable to suggest that the activities of which those described in earlier chapters form a part could come to occupy a more prominent part in the lives of many people.

Already a substantial and growing minority of the population are actively involved through voluntary organisations in caring for each other and in promoting the welfare of their communities. The forms of this involvement and the organisations through which it takes place are numerous and varied. They provide channels for the expression of strong individual commitments, for a more diffuse willingness to help and for doing something about problems directly experienced by individuals themselves. By these means a significant addition is made to the resources

available for social service purposes. But the contribution is
not only quantitative. The voluntary sector is a source of new
developments, of criticism and pressure, and a medium for
taking action where statutory agencies (for the time being at
any rate) fear to tread. Being smaller, more flexible, with
fewer bureaucratic constraints, voluntary organisations can
often help in more responsive and personal ways.

A part of the voluntary sector, probably for most people
the best-known part, consists of national organisations
mainly dependent on paid staff which occupy a specialised
niche in the overall pattern of service provision. But in most
localities such organisations are not prominent; there the
voluntary sector is predominantly composed of a multitude
of voluntary service and mutual aid groups, backed up in a
few cases by paid staff usually supported out of statutory
grants. In the field of the social services organised mutual aid
is largely a post-war phenomenon, a product of the welfare
state rather than something rendered obsolete by it.

In only a few situations is the voluntary sector an
alternative to the statutory sector, either in the sense of
offering a choice of services or in the sense of being able to
do the work now done by the statutory services. Thus
voluntary organisations are not a challenge to the state in the
sense of being able to supplant it or carry on in parallel to it.
The basic structural framework of the services, decisions
about priorities in the allocation of resources and about levels
and standards of provision, lie with the state. The voluntary
sector does influence and criticise these decisions, though in
the three towns it did seem that the statutory sector had
more influence on the voluntary sector than vice versa.
Nevertheless the existence of this framework and the now
developed capability of government both nationally and
locally to plan and, within the constraints stemming from
lack of resources and the limitations of bureaucratic action,
to implement such plans means that the voluntary sector has
come to occupy the extension ladder role advocated by the
Webbs. In this situation new questions about the relative roles
of voluntary and statutory sectors need to be asked.

Two models have been delineated to help to answer these
questions. One sees the voluntary sector as essentially
marginal, useful for minor problems and in emergencies. This

is the model most widely, if tacitly, subscribed to today. It recognises that a structure is needed and that only through the state can such a structure be established, since the state is the source of legislation and of finance. This is its strong point. It allows the voluntary sector a vanguard role, developing and opening up the path for the forward march of the state, while also accepting a subsidiary contribution from the voluntary worker. It is optimistic about the potentialities of statutory action and does not recognise limits on its capabilities, other than those of resources and public opinion. Thus its answer to problems is the growth of statutory action, the main instrument for this being increased numbers of professional staff. But here lie its weaknesses. First, there always is and will be a gap between needs and resources and hence a strong argument for mobilising as much support as possible from voluntary and informal sources. Second, a set of bureaucratically organised professional services is not omniscient and omnicompetent. It necessarily reflects the interests and ideological preconceptions of the professional and political groups which control the system, and is subject to constraints over and above those set by the politicans who are formally its masters.

The second model sees the voluntary sector as a more integral and pervasive factor in social provision. It rests on reservations about what the state can do and optimistic propositions about the potentialities of voluntary action. On this view the job of the state is to provide a framework, but not to care directly for everyone from the cradle to the grave or to respond itself to every personal problem that emerges. It is unreal to think the state can be so bounteous, caring and wise; and in so far as it purports to be so, it limits the scope for philanthropic action and mutual aid and turns itself into the target for insatiable demands. Hence the second model pins its faith to the integration of different sources of care, and calls for a shift in the balance of statutory services from direct provision towards enabling and promoting. By so doing, it can be claimed, more resources would be mobilised and a more healthy relationship achieved between statutory action and community initiatives. This model has an affinity with the pluralist approach advocated by Beveridge.

A third model, not hitherto discussed, should also be

recognised. It is one based on the belief that the state should minimise its responsibilities and leave provision for social welfare as much as possible to self-help, private charity and the commercial sector. Though it is not easy to envisage exactly how this model might be applied in present circumstances, pursued to its logical conclusion it is the doctrine of the parallel bars resuscitated. Certainly the same sort of objections apply as those adduced by the Webbs. It is difficult to see how, without a great deal of encouragement from the state, the voluntary sector could become strong enough to overcome the weaknesses evident in the earlier part of the century. And as soon as one talks about a great deal of encouragement — to extend coverage, improve standards, fill gaps and so on — it is the integral model that is being discussed.

In so far as the statutory services in the three towns were influenced by a general view of the role of other sectors in relation to their own, it seemed to be the marginal model that guided their thinking. In a few instances, for example in connection with playgroups, with aspects of the youth and adult education service and with one or two developments in the care of the elderly and the handicapped, a more integrated approach was being attempted. But for the most part voluntary services were only marginal, offering pioneering services or something ancillary, like holidays and recreation for the elderly. Efforts to strengthen and relate to voluntary and, even more so, informal sources of care were not an integral part of the work of the statutory services. They involved little staff time, quite minor sums in grant aid and were certainly not part of a thought-out strategy. There are examples outside the three towns of more developed attempts to involve the community; but in recent years reorganisation and the pressure of increasing demands have nearly everywhere absorbed most of the creative energies of the statutory health and personal social services.

This book is in no sense an attempt to propound a new plan. Hence it concludes only with a few reflections on the feasibility of an alternative approach. The strong role the statutory services have come to play in this country means that there are good foundations upon which new patterns could be developed. The growth in the voluntary sector that was indicated in Chapter 4 and the trends in the economy alluded to in this chapter also suggest that favourable conditions exist for the pursuit of an alternative, integral model. Equally, though, new patterns can hardly evolve unless they are actively supported by the state. Indeed they will require major changes in the deployment of resources and in the ways in which professional staff and politicians conceive their role. These will hardly come about serendipitously or simply by pruning statutory services. A strong policy will be needed. Here is the rub. Given the firm anchorage of the two main political parties in private enterprise on the one hand and state collectivism on the other, the prospects for the growth of a constituency that would generate the necessary impetus for change are uncertain.

## Notes

1.    Outer Circle Policy Unit, *Policing the Hidden Economy: the Significance and Control of Fiddles* (Outer Circle Policy Unit, 1978).
2.    David Freud, 'A Guide to Underground Economics', *Financial Times,* 9 April 1979.

# INDEX